cute knitted animals

Adorable patterns for birds, jungle animals, ocean creatures, and more

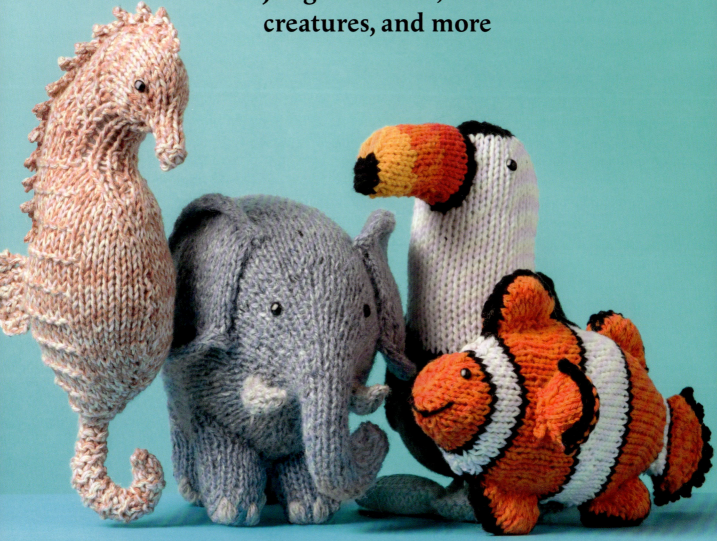

Sue Stratford

CICO BOOKS

This book is dedicated to my wonderful children Joe, Sam, Daisy, Poppy, and Lola, and Lucy who has become part of our family.

Published in 2025 by CICO Books
An imprint of Ryland Peters & Small Ltd
20–21 Jockey's Fields   1452 Davis Bugg Road
London WC1R 4BW   Warrenton, NC 27589
www.rylandpeters.com
Email: euregulations@rylandpeters.com

10 9 8 7 6 5 4 3 2 1

Text © Sue Stratford 2025
Design, illustration, and photography © CICO Books 2025

The designs in this book are copyright and must not be knitted for sale.

The author's moral rights have been asserted. All rights reserved. No part of this publication may be reproduced, stored in a retrieval system, or transmitted in any form or by any means, electronic, mechanical, photocopying, or otherwise, without the prior permission of the publisher.

A CIP record for this book is available from the British Library.
US Library of Congress CIP data has been applied for.

ISBN: 978 1 80065 425 9

Printed in China

Editor: Marie Clayton
Pattern checker: Marilyn Wilson
Designer: Alison Fenton
Photographer: Geoff Dann
Stylist: Nel Haynes
Illustrator: Stephen Dew

In-house editor: Jenny Dye
Art director: Sally Powell
Creative director: Leslie Harrington
Head of production: Patricia Harrington
Publishing manager: Carmel Edmonds

The authorised representative in the EEA is Authorised Rep Compliance Ltd., Ground Floor, 71 Lower Baggot Street, Dublin, D01 P593, Ireland
www.arccompliance.com

Note: If you are making a project for a young child, substitute the safety eyes with embroidery in yarn (see page 142).

contents

Introduction 4

Chapter 1
savannas, grasslands, and deserts 6

peanut the elephant 8
cactus the camel 12
hopper the kangaroo 15
ziggy the zebra 20
noodle the giraffe 24
tank the tortoise 28
growly the lion 30

Chapter 2
forests and jungles 34

rainbow the chameleon 36
huggy the orangutan 39
honey the sun bear 42
mischief the chimpanzee 46
bandit the ring-tailed lemur 50
dumpling the panda 54
saber the tiger 58
snoozy the sloth 62
ozzy the koala bear 65
buddy the reindeer 68
slither the scarlet king snake 72

Chapter 3
oceans, rivers, and lakes 74

bubbles the flamingo 76
chilly the polar bear 80
waddle the penguin 84
snapper the crocodile 87
splashy the whale 90
pudding the hippo 93
ribbet the frog 96
smiler the axolotl 99
twinkle the starfish 102
inky the octopus 104
neptune the seahorse 106
coco the clownfish 108

Chapter 4
skies and trees 110

shadow the bat 112
tango the toucan 116
piper the pelican 120
apollo the owl 124
binky the parrot 128

Techniques 132
Abbreviations and Acknowledgments 143
Index and Suppliers 144

introduction

Which animal is your favorite? As I designed and knitted the animals in this book, each one became my favorite. Now they are all knitted and I see them together, I cannot pick just one.

When we came up with the idea of 35 knitted animals I thought, *I'll never think of that many animals to knit*. Turns out I was wrong because there are many more creatures I could have chosen.

For some of the animals it is the yarn that makes them, such as the super-fluffy yarn I used for the orangutan and flamingo, or the color-changing yarn for the chameleon. I really enjoyed sourcing the materials for these projects and you can make them your own with the yarn you decide to use.

I always spend a lot of time creating the face of each animal as this is what gives them their character—you can make them look happy, cute, and friendly with well-placed eyes and a carefully embroidered mouth. When you embroider the mouth, if it is not right the first time, just try again.

I used a few different techniques for the animals: colorwork (intarsia and Fair Isle), essential for animals like the tiger; bobbles, which brought the octopus to life; the applied i-cord technique used for the elephant ears and bat wings which makes them more structured; and finally, my favorite technique, German short row shaping. Just remember that this technique is purely a way of turning around in the middle of the row without leaving a hole or gap in your knitting. It is easy to master and really helps create the three-dimensional shapes of the animals.

When you are finishing your animal, take your time over the sewing up. I see this as a separate project, as it is when the animal starts to come to life. A common mistake is over-stuffing and for some of the animals, you will stuff the feet but not the legs, for example, which means the legs will be flexible and "dangly."

If you aren't giving an animal to a small child, you could thread a chenille stick (pipe cleaner) along a tail so you can bend it to into a curly shape, and use floristry wire or craft wire to add structure to an animal to allow it to stand up. You can either insert the wire into the finished piece or add it during the construction process.

I hope you enjoy making your new cute friends as much as I enjoyed designing them.

Before you begin

If you are new to knitting, all the techniques you will need are covered on pages 132–143, and the abbreviations are explained on page 143. Each project has a skill rating, from Easy (one star) to Intermediate (two stars) and Advanced (three stars). Start with the Easy patterns and then move onto the next two levels once you are familiar with the basic techniques.

Chapter 1
savannas, grasslands, and deserts

Skill Level ★★★

peanut the elephant

This magnificent elephant is knitted in one piece from the tip of the trunk to the back of the body. The trunk is shaped using short rows to give it a lovely curl. The ears are made with an applied i-cord, which enhances their shape and gives them structure.

Yarn and materials
Rowan Felted Tweed (50% wool, 25% viscose, 25% alpaca) light worsted (DK) weight yarn, 191yd (175m) per 1¾oz (50g) ball
  ¾ ball of Scree 165 (gray) (MC)
  ¹⁄₁₆ ball of Clay 177 (off-white) (CC)
Pair of 6mm black domed safety eyes
Toy filling

Needles and equipment
US 2 or 3 (3mm) knitting needles
US 2 or 3 (3mm) double-pointed needles (DPNs)
Stitch markers
Crochet hook
Yarn needle
Scissors
Pins

Finished size
Head to tail: 6¼in (16cm)
Height: 5½in (14cm)

Gauge (tension)
Approx 26 sts to 4in (10cm) measured over stockinette (stocking) stitch using US 2 or 3 (3mm) knitting needles.

Abbreviations
See page 143.

Trunk, head, and body
Start at trunk.
Using MC, cast on 8 sts.
Starting with a k row, work 4 rows in st st.
Row 5: Purl (this row forms fold line).
Row 6: P1, [M1, p2] 3 times, M1, p1. (12 sts)
Starting with a k row, work 4 rows in st st.
Shaping is done with short rows (see page 140).
*Row 11: K9, turn.
Row 12: Slds, p5, turn.
Row 13: Slds, k to end.
Row 14: Purl.*
Rep from * to * 7 more times.
Row 43: [K2, M1] 5 times, k2. (17 sts)
Row 44: Purl.
Row 45: K13, turn.
Row 46: Slds, p7, turn.
Row 47: Slds, k to end.
Row 48: Purl.
Row 49: [K2, M1] 4 times, k1, [M1, k2] 4 times. (25 sts)
Row 50: Purl.
Row 51: K20, turn.
Row 52: Slds, p14, turn.
Row 53: Slds, k to end.
Row 54: Purl.
Row 55: [K2, M1] 6 times, k1, [M1, k2] 6 times. (37 sts)
Row 56: Purl.
Row 57: K30, turn.
Row 58: Slds, p22, turn.
Row 59: Slds, k to end.
Row 60: Purl.

Row 61: [K2, M1] 9 times, k1, [M1, k2] 9 times. (55 sts)
Row 62: Purl.
Row 63: K45, turn.
Row 64: Slds, p34, turn.
Row 65: Slds, k28, turn.
Row 66: Slds, p22, turn.
Row 67: Slds, k16, turn.
Row 68: Slds, p10, turn.
Row 69: Slds, k to end.
Row 70: Purl.
Row 71: K2, [M1, k3] 7 times, k9, [M1, k3] 7 times, k2. (69 sts)
Row 72: Purl.
Row 73: K4, turn.
Row 74: Slds, p to end.
Row 75: K3, turn.
Row 76: Slds, p to end.
Row 77: Knit.
Row 78: P4, turn.
Row 79: Slds, k to end.
Row 80: P3, turn.
Row 81: Slds, k to end.
Starting with a p row, work 7 rows in st st.
Row 89: K30, ssk, PM, k5, PM, k2tog, k30. (67 sts)
Row 90: Purl.
Row 91: K to 2 sts before marker, ssk, SM, k to marker, SM, k2tog, k to end. (65 sts)
Row 92: Purl.
Rep Rows 91 and 92 once more. (63 sts)
Starting with a k row, work 18 rows in st st, SM on each row.
Row 113: K to 2 sts before marker, ssk, SM, k to marker, SM, k2tog, k to end. (61 sts)

8   savannas, grasslands, and deserts

Starting with a p row, work 3 rows in st st.
Row 117: K2, ssk, k to 2 sts before marker, ssk, SM, k to marker, SM, k2tog, k to last 4 sts, k2tog, k2. (*57 sts*)
Row 118: Purl.
Rep Rows 117 and 118 three more times. (*45 sts*)
Move markers one st out each side so there are 8 sts between markers.
Row 125: K2, ssk, k to marker, SM, ssk, k to 2 sts before marker, k2tog, SM, k to last 4 sts, k2tog, k2. (*41 sts*)
Row 126: P to marker, SM, p2tog, p2, p2togtbl, SM, p to end. (*39 sts*)
Row 127: K to 1 st before marker, RM, CDD, RM, k to end. (*37 sts*)
Arrange first 13 sts on one DPN and rem 14 sts on a second. Hold with RS tog and using third needle, bind (cast) off using three-needle bind (cast) off technique (see page 139) to last st, k1 and bind (cast) off.

Left leg
(make two)
*Using MC, cast on 4 sts.
Row 1 (WS): Purl.
Row 2: K1, M1, k2, M1, k1. (*6 sts*)
Row 3: P1, M1, p4, M1, p1. (*8 sts*)
Starting with a k row, work 2 rows in st st.
Row 6: K1, ssk, k2, k2tog, k1. (*6 sts*)
Row 7: P1, p2tog, p2togtbl, p1. (*4 sts*)
Cont working in st st and cast on 7 sts at beg of next 2 rows. (*18 sts*)
Starting with a k row, work 6 rows in st st.*
Row 16: Bind (cast) off 1 st, k to end. (*17 sts*)
Row 17: Bind (cast) off 10 sts, p to end. (*7 sts*)
**Row 18: K1, ssk, k1, k2tog, k1. (*5 sts*)
Row 19: Purl.
Row 20: Ssk, k1, k2tog. (*3 sts*)
Row 21: Purl.
Bind (cast) off.

Right leg
(make two)
Work as for left leg from * to *.
Row 16: Bind (cast) off 10 sts, k to end. (*8 sts*)
Row 17: Bind (cast) off 1 st, p to end. (*7 sts*)
Work from ** to end.

Ear
(make two)
Made using applied i-cord technique (see page 134) as foll:
Using MC and DPNs, cast on 3 sts.
I-cord row 1: K3, push sts to other end of needle, pulling yarn firmly across back of work, without turning.
Rep i-cord row 1 twenty-three more times. Slide the three stitches to the end of your needle and knit them together.

Use a crochet hook to pick up 18 sts along row edge of i-cord (pick up 2 sts from 2 rows, miss 1 row to end). (*19 sts*)
Shaping is done with short rows.
Row 1: P10, turn.
Row 2: Slds, k3, turn.
Row 3: Slds, p4, turn.
Row 4: Slds, k6, turn.
Row 5: Slds, p7, turn.
Row 6: Slds, k8, turn.
Row 7: Slds, p10, turn.
Row 8: Slds, k11, turn.
Row 9: Slds, p13, turn.
Row 10: Slds, k14, turn.
Row 11: Slds, p to last 3 sts, sl3 wyif.
Row 12: Knit.
Row 13: P to last 3 sts, sl3 wyif.
Rep Rows 12 and 13 seven more times.
Row 28: K14, turn.
Row 29: Slds, p10, sl3 wyif.
Row 30: K12, turn.
Row 31: Slds, p8, turn.
Row 32: Slds, k6, turn.
Row 33: Slds, p6, sl3 wyif.
Row 34: K2, k2tog, k4, turn. (*18 sts*)
Row 35: Slds, p3, sl3 wyif.
Row 36: K2, k2tog, turn. (*17 sts*)
Row 37: Sl3 wyif.
Rep Rows 36 and 37 once more. (*16 sts*)
Row 40: K2, k2tog, k9, turn. (*15 sts*)
Row 41: Slds, p7, turn.
Row 42: Slds, k5, turn.

10 savannas, grasslands, and deserts

Row 43: Slds, p6, sl3 wyif.
Row 44: K2, k2tog, turn. (*14 sts*)
Row 45: Sl3 wyif.
Row 46: K2, k2tog, turn. (*13 sts*)
Rep Rows 45 and 46 until 3 sts rem.
Thread yarn through rem sts to fasten off, leaving length of yarn for sewing up.

Tail
Using MC, cast on 4 sts.
Row 1: K4, push sts to other end of needle, pulling yarn firmly across back of work, without turning.
Rep Row 1 five more times.
Row 7: K1, k2tog, k1. (*3 sts*)
Row 8: K3, push sts to other end of needle, pulling yarn firmly across back of work, without turning.
Rep Row 8 three more times.
Thread yarn through rem sts to fasten off.

Tusk
(make two)
Shaping is done with short rows.
Using CC and DPNs, cast on 6 sts.
Row 5: K6, turn.
Row 6: Slds, p3, turn.
Row 7: Slds, k to end.
Row 8: Purl.
Row 9: K1, ssk, k2tog, k1. (*4 sts*)
Row 10: Purl.
Thread yarn through rem sts to fasten off, leaving a length of yarn for sewing up.

Making up
Using MC and starting at the trunk, sew the seam from the end of the trunk to the fold line, then fold over so that this section will be inside the trunk. Continue sewing the seam along the trunk, stuffing with toy filling as you go. The trunk will curl as you sew and stuff it. Pin the head together and stuff with toy filling. Using the photos as a guide for position, push each of the eyes through the knitting. Once you are happy with their placement, remove the pins and toy filling and push the backs of the eyes firmly onto the post of each eye. Replace the toy filling. Continue sewing the seam along the bottom of the head and body, stuffing with toy filling as you go. Before closing the seam check the amount of toy filling is enough to give the head and body definition.

Sew the small side seam at the back of each leg, and fold and sew the base of the foot in place. Repeat for the three other legs. Place some toy filling inside each leg and pin in place to the body, adding more toy filling as needed and using the photos for guidance. Sew each leg and foot in place.

Carefully steam the ears with an iron, without pressing the iron on the knitting. This will give the ears a better shape and stop them from curling. Using the photos for guidance, pin the ears in place. When you are happy with their placement, sew them in place along the front edge of the ear.

Using CC, sew the seam along the edge of the tusk, placing a small amount of toy filling inside. Repeat for the second tusk. Pin each tusk in place, making sure they are level. When you are happy with their placement, sew each tusk securely to the face.

To make the fluffy end of the tail, thread a yarn needle with a double length of yarn and sew from the base of the tail up inside, then thread the needle back down so that there are now four strands of yarn at the bottom of the tail, plus the bound- (cast-) off length. Separate out the strands of each piece of yarn and trim to length. Sew the tail to the body.

Using a double strand of CC yarn, embroider three toes on each foot with chain stitches (see page 142), starting from the base of the foot. Work one straight stitch (see page 142) in the center of each chain stitch.

peanut the elephant 11

Skill Level ★ ★ ★

cactus the camel

This little camel is an easy knit, with just one color throughout and basic increases and decreases. Did you know that camel humps store fat, not water like people usually assume?

Yarn and materials
Rico Ricorumi Spray DK (100% cotton) light worsted (DK) weight yarn, 62yd (57.5m) per ⅞oz (25g) ball
   2¼ balls of Beige 008 (MC)
Rico Ricorumi DK (100% cotton) light worsted (DK) weight yarn, 63yd (58m) per ⅞oz (25g) ball
   ¾ ball of Nougat 056 (brown) (CC)
Small amount of black fingering (4-ply) yarn
Pair of 5mm black domed safety eyes
Toy filling

Needles and equipment
US 2 or 3 (3mm) knitting needles
Pair of US 2 or 3 (3mm) double-pointed knitting needles (DPNs) for i-cord technique
Two spare knitting needles
Yarn needle
Scissors
Pins

Finished size
Nose to rear: 8¼in (21cm)
Top of head to sole of foot: 8¾in (22cm)

Gauge (tension)
Approx 26 sts to 4in (10cm) measured over stockinette (stocking) stitch using US 2 or 3 (3mm) knitting needles.

Abbreviations
See page 143.

Neck
Start at top of neck (neck is worked in two halves).
SIDE 1
Using MC, cast on 9 sts.
Rows 1–10: Starting with a k row, work in st st.
Row 11: K1, M1, k to end. (*10 sts*)
Row 12: Purl.
Break yarn and place sts on a spare needle.
SIDE 2
Using MC, cast on 9 sts.
Rows 1–10: Starting with a k row, work in st st.
Row 11: K to last st, M1, k1. (*10 sts*)
Row 12: Purl.
Break yarn and place sts on a spare needle.

Body
Using MC, cast on 8 sts.
Row 1: Purl.
Row 2: K1, [M1, k2] 3 times, M1, k1. (*12 sts*)
Row 3: Purl.
Row 4: K1, M1, k4, M1, k2, M1, k4, M1, k1. (*16 sts*)
Row 5: P1, M1, p6, M1, p2, M1, p6, M1, p1. (*20 sts*)
Row 6: K1, M1, k8, M1, k2, M1, k8, M1, k1. (*24 sts*)
Row 7: Purl.
Row 8: K1, M1, k10, M1, k2, M1, k10, M1, k1. (*28 sts*)
Row 9: P1, M1, p12, M1, p2, M1, p12, M1, p1. (*32 sts*)
Row 10: K1, M1, k14, M1, k2, M1, k14, M1, k1.
Row 11: Purl.
Row 12: K1, M1, k16, M1, k2, M1, k16, M1, k1.
Row 13: Purl.
Row 14: K1, M1, k18, M1, k2, M1, k18, M1, k1.
Row 15: Purl.

Row 16: K1, M1, k20, M1, k2, M1, k20, M1, k1.
Row 17: Purl.
Row 18: K1, M1, k22, M1, k2, M1, k22, M1, k1.
Row 19: Purl.
Row 20: K1, M1, k to last st, M1, k1. (*54 sts*)
Row 21: Purl.
Join neck to body.
Row 22: With RS facing, k across side 1 of neck, side 2 of neck. (*76 sts*)
Row 23: Purl.
Row 24: K1, M1, k37, M1, k37, M1, k1. (*79 sts*)
Starting with a p row, work 9 rows in st st.
Row 34: K36, ssk, k3, k2tog, k36. (*77 sts*)
Row 35: Purl.
Row 36: K1, ssk, k32, ssk, k3, k2tog, k32, k2tog, k1. (*73 sts*)
Row 37: Purl.
Row 38: K1, ssk, k30, ssk, k3, k2tog, k30, k2tog, k1. (*69 sts*)
Row 39: Purl.
Row 40: Bind (cast) off 5 sts, then k24, bind (cast) off 10 sts, then k24 sts, bind (cast) off 5 sts. (*two groups of 25 sts*)
With WS facing, rejoin yarn to one group of sts, starting with a p row, work 7 rows in st st.
Leave these sts on a spare needle.
With WS facing, rejoin yarn to second group of 25 sts, starting with a p row, work 7 rows in st st. With both sections RS together and using a third needle, bind (cast) off using three-needle bind (cast) off technique (see page 139).

Head
Using MC, cast on 8 sts.
Row 1: K1, [M1, k2] 3 times, M1, k1. (*12 sts*)
Row 2: Purl.

12   **savannas, grasslands, and deserts**

Row 3: K1, M1, k4, M1, k2, M1, k4, M1, k1. (*16 sts*)
Row 4: Purl.
Row 5: K1, M1, k6, M1, k2, M1, k6, M1, k1. (*20 sts*)
Row 6: Purl.
Row 7: K1, M1, k8, M1, k2, M1, k8, M1, k1. (*24 sts*)
Row 8: Purl.
Row 9: K1, M1, k10, M1, k2, M1, k10, M1, k1. (*28 sts*)
Starting with a p row, work 7 rows in st st.
Row 17: K2, ssk, k to last 4 sts, k2tog, k2. (*26 sts*)
Row 18: Purl.
Rep last 2 rows twice more. (*22 sts*)
Starting with a k row, work 2 rows in st st.
Row 25: K2, ssk, k4, ssk, k2, k2tog, k4, k2tog, k2. (*18 sts*)
Row 26: Purl.
Row 27: K2, ssk, k2, ssk, k2, k2tog, k2, k2tog, k2. (*14 sts*)
Divide rem sts evenly between two needles and, with RS tog and using third needle, bind (cast) off using three-needle bind (cast) off technique.

Leg and foot
(make 4)
Using MC, cast on 13 sts.
Starting with a k row, work 19 rows in st st. Break MC, join in CC.
Row 20: Purl.
Row 21: K1, M1, k4, M1, k3, M1, k4, M1, k1. (*17 sts*)
Row 22: Purl.
Row 23: K1, M1, k6, M1, k3, M1, k6, M1, k1. (*21 sts*)
Starting with a p row, work 4 rows in st st.
Row 28: Bind (cast) off 7 sts, k to end. (*14 sts*)
Row 29: Bind (cast) off 7 sts, p to end. (*7 sts*)
Starting with a k row, work 4 rows in st st.
Row 34: K1, ssk, k1, k2tog, k1. *(5 sts)*
Row 35: Purl.
Bind (cast) off.

Ear
(make 2)
Using MC, cast on 6 sts.
Starting with a k row, work 4 rows in st st.
Row 5: K5, turn.
Row 6: Slds, p3, turn.
Row 7: Slds, k to end.
Row 8: Purl.
Row 9: K1, ssk, k2tog, k1. (*4 sts*)
Starting with a p row, work 7 rows in st st.
Bind (cast) off.

Tail
Using DPNs and MC, cast on 4 sts.
Row 1: K4, push sts to other end of needle, pulling yarn firmly across back of work, without turning.
Rep Row 1 until tail measures 1½in (4cm).
Thread yarn through rem sts to fasten off, leaving length of yarn for sewing up.

Making up
Pin the head together and stuff with toy filling. Using the photos as a guide for position, push the safety eyes through the knitting. When you are happy with their placement, remove the pins and toy filling and firmly push the back onto the post of each eye. Re-stuff the head.

Starting at the base of the body, gather the cast-on edge and sew along the seam to the tail. Stuff the body with toy filling. Sew the seam across the back of the body, adding more toy filling as necessary. Continue sewing the seam along the neck, stuffing with toy filling as you go. Sew the top of the seam closed. Pin the head to the top of the neck, making sure there is enough toy filling in the neck to support it. Sew the head in place.

Sew the first side seam on the foot, stuff with a small amount of toy filling to add definition, then sew the second seam closed. Sew the leg seam. Pin each leg in place, using the photos as a guide and with the bound- (cast-) off edge of the foot underneath and the leg seam at the back. Sew in place.

To make the fluffy end of the tail, thread a yarn needle with a double length of MC and sew from the cast-on end of the tail up inside, leave about 1in (2.5cm) hanging, then thread the needle back down. Repeat so that there are now eight strands of yarn at the bottom of the tail plus the bound- (cast-) off length. Separate out the ply of each piece of yarn and trim to length. Sew around the end of the tail to secure the loose ends. Sew the tail to the body.

Using A, sew two chain stitches to make the nose and embroider the mouth using backstitch (see page 142).

14   savannas, grasslands, and deserts

Skill Level ★★★

hopper the kangaroo

This loving kangaroo with her little Joey has a built-in pocket to use as a pouch. Little Joey is a miniature version of Mom. Did you know that kangaroos are left-handed?

Yarn and materials
Rowan Felted Tweed (50% wool, 25% viscose, 25% alpaca) light worsted (DK) weight yarn, 191yd (175m) per 1¾oz (50g) ball
  1 ball of Camel 157 (light brown) (MC)
  Small amount of Phantom 153 (dark brown) (CC)

Pair of 5mm black domed safety eyes

Pair of 3mm black beads

Black cotton sewing thread

Toy filling

Needles and equipment
US 2 or 3 (3mm) knitting needles

US 2 or 3 (3mm) double-pointed needles (DPNs)

Spare knitting needle for three-needle bind (cast) off

2 stitch holders or spare yarn

Stitch markers

Yarn needle

Beading needle

Scissors

Pins

Finished size
Base to top of head excluding ears: 6¾in (17cm)

Gauge (tension)
Approx 26 sts to 4in (10cm) measured over stockinette (stocking) stitch using US 2 or 3 (3mm) knitting needles.

Abbreviations
See page 143.

Back of pouch lining
Using MC, cast on 13 sts.
Starting with a k row, work 18 rows in st st.
Break yarn and place sts on a spare piece of yarn.

Main kangaroo body and tail
Starting with the base.
Using MC, cast on 3 sts.
Starting with a p row, work 3 rows in st st.
Row 4: [K1, M1] twice, k1. (*5 sts*)
Starting with a p row, work 3 rows in st st.
Row 8: K1, M1, k to last st, M1, k1. (*7 sts*)
Row 9: P1, M1, p to last st, M1, p1. (*9 sts*)
Rep last 2 rows three more times. (*21 sts*)
Starting with a k row, work 12 rows in st st.
Row 28: K1, ssk, k to last 3 sts, k2tog, k1. (*19 sts*)
Row 29: Purl.
Rep last 2 rows once more. (*17 sts*)

Shape for tail.
Row 32: Cast on 30 sts, k to end. (*47 sts*)
Row 33: Cast on 30 sts, p to end. (*77 sts*)
Row 34: K35, M1, k7, M1, k35. (*79 sts*)
Row 35: Purl.
Row 36: K36, M1, k7, M1, k36. (*81 sts*)
Shaping is done with short rows (see page 140).
Row 37: P78, turn.
Row 38: Slds, k33, M1, k7, M1, k34, turn. (*83 sts*)
Row 39: Slds, p71, turn.
Row 40: Slds, k66, turn.
Row 41: Slds, p61, turn.
Row 42: Slds, k56, turn.
Row 43: Slds, p51, place rem 18 sts onto st holder for tail. (*65 sts left*)
Row 44: Slds, k46, place rem 18 sts onto st holder for tail. (*47 sts left*)
Row 45: Purl.

hopper the kangaroo 15

Row 46: K1, ssk, k15, ssk, k7, k2tog, k15, k2tog, k1. (*43 sts*)
Row 47: Purl.
Row 48: K1, ssk, k13, ssk, k7, k2tog, k13, k2tog, k1. (*39 sts*)
Row 49: Purl.
Row 50: K13, place next 13 sts on spare yarn, with RS facing k across 13 held back of pouch lining sts, k13. (*39 sts*)
Place back of pouch lining.
Starting with a p row, work 5 rows in st st.
Row 56: K10, ssk, k1, k2tog, k9, ssk, k1, k2tog, k10. (*35 sts*)
Starting with a p row, work 3 rows in st st.
Row 60: K9, ssk, k1, k2tog, k7, ssk, k1, k2tog, k9. (*31 sts*)
Row 61: Purl.
Row 62: K8, ssk, k1, k2tog, k5, ssk, k1, k2tog, k8. (*27 sts*)
Row 63: Purl.
Row 64: K7, ssk, k1, k2tog, k3, ssk, k1, k2tog, k7. (*23 sts*)
Row 65: Purl.
Row 66: K6, ssk, k1, k2tog, k1, ssk, k1, k2tog, k6. (*19 sts*)
Row 67: Purl.
Bind (cast) off.
Slip each set of tail sts onto separate needles. With RS tog and using third needle, bind (cast) off using three-needle bind (cast) off technique (see page 139).
FRONT OF POUCH LINING
With RS facing, sl 13 sts held on spare yarn onto a needle. Rejoin yarn and, starting with a k row, work 16 rows in st st. Bind (cast) off.

Main kangaroo left leg and foot
Using MC, cast on 14 sts.
Starting with a k row, work 8 rows in st st.
Shaping is done with short rows.
Row 9: Bind (cast) off 6 sts, then k6, turn. (*8 sts*)
Row 10: Slds, p4, turn.
Row 11: Slds, k3, turn.
Row 12: Slds, p2, turn.
Row 13: Slds, k to end.
Row 14: Purl.
Row 15: Cast on 5 sts, k7, M1, k5, M1, k1. (*15 sts*)
Starting with a p row, work 13 rows in st st.
Row 29: K1, ssk, k2, k2tog, k1, ssk, k2, k2tog, k1. (*11 sts*)
Row 30: P1, p2tog, p2togtbl, p1, p2tog, p2togtbl, p1. (*7 sts*)
Arrange first 4 sts on one DPN and rem 3 sts on a second. Hold with RS tog and using third needle, bind (cast) off using three-needle bind (cast) off technique to last st, k1 and bind (cast) off.

Main kangaroo right leg and foot
Using MC, cast on 14 sts.
Starting with a k row, work 7 rows in st st.
Shaping is done with short rows.
Row 8: Bind (cast) off 6 sts, then p6, turn. (*8 sts*)
Row 9: Slds, k4, turn.
Row 10: Slds, p3, turn.
Row 11: Slds, k2, turn.
Row 12: Slds, p to end.
Row 13: Knit.
Row 14: Cast on 5 sts, p7, M1, p5, M1, p1. (*15 sts*)

Starting with a k row, work 13 rows in st st.
Row 28: P1, p2tog, p2, p2togtbl, p1, p2tog, p2, p2togtbl, p1. (*11 sts*)
Row 29: K1, ssk, k2tog, k1, ssk, k2tog, k1. (*7 sts*)
Arrange first 4 sts on one DPN and rem 3 sts on a second. Hold with RS tog and using third needle, bind (cast) off using three-needle bind (cast) off technique to last st, k1 and bind (cast) off.

Main kangaroo head
Using MC, cast on 9 sts.
Row 1: Purl.
Row 2: K1, M1, k3, M1, k1, M1, k3, M1, k1. (*13 sts*)
Row 3: Purl.
Row 4: K1, M1, k4, M1, k3, M1, k4, M1, k1. (*17 sts*)
Row 5: Purl.
Row 6: K7, M1, k3, M1, k7. (*19 sts*)
Row 7: Purl.
Row 8: K8, M1, k3, M1, k8. (*21 sts*)
Row 9: Purl.
Row 10: K9, M1, k3, M1, k9. (*23 sts*)
Starting with a p row, work 3 rows in st st.
Row 14: K10, M1, k3, M1, k10. (*25 sts*)
Row 15: P11, M1, p3, M1, p11. (*27 sts*)
Row 16: K12, M1, k3, M1, k12. (*29 sts*)
Row 17: P13, M1, p3, M1, p13. (*31 sts*)
Starting with a k row, work 4 rows in st st.
Row 22: K12, ssk, k3, k2tog, k12. (*29 sts*)
Row 23: P11, p2tog, p3, p2togtbl, p11. (*27 sts*)
Row 24: K2, ssk, k6, ssk, k3, k2tog, k6, k2tog, k2. (*23 sts*)
Row 25: P2, p2tog, p5, p2tog, p1, p2togtbl, p5, p2togtbl, p2. (*19 sts*)
Arrange first 10 sts on one DPN and rem 9 sts on a second. Hold with RS tog and using third needle, bind (cast) off using three-needle bind (cast) off technique to last st, k1 and bind (cast) off.

Main kangaroo outer ear
Using MC, cast on 5 sts.
Starting with a k row, work 4 rows in st st.
Row 5: Ssk, k1, k2tog. (*3 sts*)
Row 6: CDD. (*1 st*)
Thread yarn through rem st to fasten off.

Main kangaroo inner ear
Using MC, cast on 4 sts.
Starting with a k row, work 4 rows in st st.
Row 5: Ssk, k2tog. (*2 sts*)
Row 6: Purl.
Thread yarn through rem sts to fasten off.

Main kangaroo left arm
Using MC, cast on 4 sts.
Row 1 (WS): Purl.
Row 2: K1, M1, k to last st, M1, k1. (*6 sts*)
Row 3: Purl.
Row 4: Cast on 6 sts, k to end. (*12 sts*)

16   savannas, grasslands, and deserts

Starting with a p row, work 7 rows in st st.
Shaping is done with short rows.
Row 12: K9, turn.
Row 13: Slds, p5, turn.
Row 14: Slds, k4, turn.
Row 15: Slds, p3, turn.
Row 16: Slds, k to end.
Starting with a p row, work 9 rows in st st.
Row 26: [K1, ssk, k2tog, k1] twice. (*8 sts*)
Row 27: Purl.
Row 28: [K2tog] four times. (*4 sts*)
Thread yarn through rem sts to fasten off, leaving length of yarn for sewing up.

Main kangaroo right arm
Using MC, cast on 4 sts.
Row 1: Knit.
Row 2: P1, M1, p2, M1, k1. (*6 sts*)
Row 3: Knit.
Row 4: Cast on 6 sts, p to end. (*12 sts*)
Starting with a k row, work 7 rows in st st.
Shaping is done with short rows.
Row 12: P9, turn.
Row 13: Slds, k5, turn.
Row 14: Slds, p4, turn.
Row 15: Slds, k3, turn.
Row 16: Slds, p to end.
Starting with a k row, work 9 rows in st st.
Row 26: [P1, p2tog, p2togtbl, p1] twice. (*8 sts*)
Row 27: Knit.
Row 28: [P2tog] four times. (*4 sts*)
Thread yarn through rem sts to fasten off, leaving length of yarn for sewing up.

Main kangaroo nose
Using CC, cast on 3 sts.
Row 1: [K1, M1] twice, k1. (*5 sts*)
Row 2: Purl.
Row 3: Ssk, k1, k2tog. (*3 sts*)
Thread yarn through rem sts to fasten off, leaving a length of yarn for sewing up.

Baby kangaroo tail and body
Using MC, cast on 3 sts.
Starting with a k row, work 4 rows in st st.
Row 5: K2, M1, k1. (*4 sts*)
Row 6: Purl.
Row 7: K2, M1, k2. (*5 sts*)
Row 8: Purl.
Row 9: K1, M1, k to last st, M1, k1. (*7 sts*)
Row 10: Purl.
Row 11: Cast on 3 sts, k to end. (*10 sts*)
Row 12: Cast on 3 sts, p to end. (*13 sts*)
Starting with a k row, work 4 rows in st st.
Row 17: K1, ssk, k to last 3 sts, k2tog, k1. (*11 sts*)
Starting with a p row, work 3 rows in st st.
Row 21: K1, ssk, k to last 3 sts, k2tog, k1. (*9 sts*)
Row 22: Purl.
Bind (cast) off, leaving a length of yarn for sewing up.

Baby kangaroo head
Using MC, cast on 6 sts.
Starting with a p row, work 3 rows in st st.
Row 4: K2, M1, k to last 2 sts, M1, k2. (*8 sts*)

18   savannas, grasslands, and deserts

Row 5: P3, M1, p to last 3 sts, M1, p3. (*10 sts*)
Starting with a k row, work 4 rows in st st.
Row 10: K1, [ssk, k2tog] twice, k1. (*6 sts*)
Divide rem sts evenly between two needles and, with RS tog and using third needle, bind (cast) off using three-needle bind (cast) off technique.

Baby kangaroo leg
(make two)
Using MC and DPNs, cast on 4 sts.
Row 1: K4, push sts to other end of needle, pulling yarn firmly across back of work, without turning.
Rep Row 1 twice.
Thread yarn through rem sts to fasten off.

Baby kangaroo arm
(make two)
Using MC and DPNs, cast on 3 sts.
Row 1: K3, push sts to other end of needle, pulling yarn firmly across back of work, without turning.
Rep Row 1 four more times.
Thread yarn through rem sts to fasten off.

Baby kangaroo ear
(make two)
Using MC, cast on 3 sts.
Starting with a k row, work 2 rows in st st.
Row 3: CDD. (*1 st*)
Thread yarn through rem st to fasten off.

Making up
Main kangaroo
Place back and front pouch lining pieces together and sew around outside edges to form a pouch.

Pin the base in place along the underside of the tail. Starting at the end of the tail, sew together and sew the base in place. Stuffing with toy filling as you go, begin to sew the seam up the back of the body, adding more filling as you work. Thread your yarn through the bound- (cast-) off stitches around the neck and gather slightly.

Starting at the bound- (cast-) off edge of the head, start sewing the seam along the bottom. Add the safety eyes to the head by pushing through the knitting using the photos as a guide for position. When you are happy with the placement, firmly push the backs onto the post of each eye. Continue sewing the seam, stuffing with toy filling as you go. Pin an outer ear and an inner ear with WS together, using the photos as a guide, and sew together. Repeat for the second ear. Pin the ears in place on the head and when you are happy with their position, sew in place. Pin the nose in place using the photos as a guide, and then sew in place. Sew the head to the body.

Starting at the fastened off end, sew the seam along the arm, stuffing with toy filling as you go. Sew the cast-on edge closed. Repeat for the second arm. Pin the arms in place with the seam underneath, then sew firmly to the body.

Sew the small seam of bound- (cast-) off and cast-on stitches on the top of the foot together to make the foot point upward. Then starting at the end of the foot, sew along the side seam, stuffing with toy filling as you go and leaving the short leg empty. Sew through the seam on top of the foot to catch together the back and front of the leg to stop the toy filling escaping, making sure the stitches don't show on the underside of the leg. Sew the cast-on edges together. Repeat for the second foot. Pin each leg and foot in place with the seam toward the inside along the front seam of the base, using the photos as a guide, then sew in place.

Using CC, embroider the mouth using backstitch (see page 142).

Baby kangaroo
Sew the seam along the front of the body, stuff with toy filling, and sew the base closed.

Place a small amount of toy filling inside the head and close the seam. Sew the head to the body. Using the photos as a guide for position, sew the arms to the body and then sew the legs in place so that they point upward. Sew the ears to the top of the head. Using black sewing thread and a beading needle, sew the bead eyes in place. Using CC, embroider the nose using straight stitches (see page 142).

hopper the kangaroo 19

Skill Level ★ ★ ★

ziggy the zebra

The black stripes of this sweet zebra are worked in reverse stockinette (stocking) stitch to give definition. The way the body is made means he will sit down nicely with his dangly legs. The mane is worked using slipped stitches, which gives a lovely result.

Yarn and materials

Rico Ricorumi DK (100% cotton) light worsted (DK) weight yarn, 63yd (58m) per 7⁄8oz (25g) ball

   1 ball of Black 060 (A)

   1 ball of White 001 (B)

Small amount of shade Rose 008 (pink) (C)

Pair of 6mm black domed safety eyes

Toy filling

Needles and equipment

US 2 or 3 (3mm) knitting needles

US 6 (4mm) knitting needle

Spare knitting needle for three-needle bind (cast) off

Yarn needle

Scissors

Pins

Finished size

Foot to top of head: 7½in (19cm)

Nose to tip of tail: 9½in (24cm)

Gauge (tension)

Approx 26 sts to 4in (10cm) measured over stockinette (stocking) stitch using US 2 or 3 (3mm) knitting needles.

Abbreviations

See page 143.

Head

Start at nose.

Using US 2 or 3 (3mm) needle and A, cast on 10 sts.

Row 1 (WS): Purl.

Row 2: K1, M1, k3, M1, k2, M1, k3, M1, k1. (*14 sts*)

Row 3: Purl.

Row 4: K1, M1, k5, M1, k2, M1, k5, M1, k1. (*18 sts*)

Row 5: Purl.

Join in B, do not break off A, carry yarn not in use along edge of knitting to work stripes. Starting with a k row, work 4 rows in st st.

Change to A, k 2 rows.

Change to B, k 1 row.

Row 13: P2, M1, p5, M1, p4, M1, p5, M1, p2. (*22 sts*)

Starting with a k row, work 2 rows in st st.

Change to A, k 1 row.

Row 17: K2, M1, k7, M1, k4, M1, k7, M1, k2. (*26 sts*)

Change to B, k 1 row.

Shaping is done with short rows (see page 140).

Row 19: P23, turn.

Row 20: Slds, k5, ssk, k4, k2tog, k6, turn.

Row 21: Slds, p13, turn.

Row 22: Slds, k9, turn.

Row 23: Slds, p6, turn.

Row 24: Slds, k3, turn.

Row 25: Slds, p to end. (*24 sts*)

Change to A, k 1 row.

Row 27: K1, ssk, k5, ssk, k4, k2tog, k5, k2tog, k1. (*20 sts*)

Change to B, k 1 row.

Row 29: P17, turn.

Row 30: Slds, k13, turn.

Row 31: Slds, p9, turn.

Row 32: Slds, k5, turn.

Row 33: Slds, p to end.

Change to A, k 2 rows.

Change to B, k 1 row.

Row 37: P9, M1, p2, M1, p6, turn.

Row 38: Slds, k15, turn.
Row 39: Slds, p10, turn.
Row 40: Slds, k5, turn.
Row 41: Slds, p to end. (*22 sts*)
Change to A, k 1 row.
Row 43: K9, M1, k4, M1, k9. (*24 sts*)
Change to B, starting with a k row, work 2 rows in st st.
Row 46: Cast on 10 sts, k across these sts, k3, using US 6 (4mm) needle, bind (cast) off 18 sts, then k2. (*one group of 13 sts, one group of 3 sts*)
Note: Binding (casting) off with larger needle means bound- (cast-) off sts are looser so will "stretch" more when sewing neck to body.
Row 47: Cast on 10 sts, p across these sts, p3, turn, cast on 4 sts, turn, p13. (*30 sts*)
Row 48: K2, M1, k9, turn.
Row 49: Slds, p10, turn.
Row 50: Slds, k5, turn.
Row 51: Slds, p to end. (*31 sts*)
Row 52: K29, turn.
Row 53: Slds, p9, turn.
Row 54: Slds, k to last 2 sts, M1, k2. (*32 sts*)
Row 55: Purl.
Change to A.
Row 56: Cast on 4 sts, k to end. (*36 sts*)
Rep last row once more. (*40 sts*)
Change to B, starting with a k row, work 4 rows in st st.
Change to A, k 2 rows.
Rep last 6 rows four more times.
Change to B, starting with a k row, work 2 rows in st st.
Row 90: Bind (cast) off 4 sts, k to end. (*36 sts*)
Row 91: Bind (cast) off 4 sts, p to end. (*32 sts*)
Row 92: K13, turn.
Row 93: Slds, p to end.
Row 94: K7, turn.
Row 95: Slds, p to end.
Row 96: Knit.
Row 97: P13, turn.
Row 98: Slds, k to end.
Row 99: P7, turn.
Row 100: Slds, k to end.
Row 101: P16, place rem 16 sts on another needle. With RS tog and using third needle, bind (cast) off using three-needle bind (cast) off technique (see page 139).

Leg and foot
(make 4)
Start at top of leg.
Using US 2 or 3 (3mm) needles and A, cast on 12 sts.
Rows 1 and 2: Knit.
Change to B, starting with a k row, work 4 rows in st st. Change to A, k 2 rows.
Rep last 6 rows once more.
Change to B, starting with a k row, work 4 rows in st st. Change to A, k 1 row.
Row 20: P5, M1, p2, M1, p5. (*14 sts*)
Row 21: Knit.
Row 22: P6, M1, p2, M1, p6. (*16 sts*)
Starting with a k row, work 2 rows in st st.
Row 25: Bind (cast) off 6 sts, k to end. (*10 sts*)
Row 26: Bind (cast) off 6 sts, p to end. (*4 sts*)
Row 27: K1, M1, k2, M1, k1. (*6 sts*)
Starting with a p row, work 3 rows in st st.
Row 31: Ssk, k2, k2tog. (*4 sts*)
Row 32: Purl.
Bind (cast) off, leaving enough yarn to sew up foot.

Tail
Using US 2 or 3 (3mm) needles and A, cast on 6 sts.
Starting with a k row, work 2 rows in st st.
Change to B, starting with a k row, work 2 rows in st st.
Rep last 4 rows twice more.
Change to A and k 1 row.
Row 14: P1, [M1, p2] twice, M1, p1. (*9 sts*)
Starting with a k row, work 3 rows in st st.
Row 18: [P1, p2tog] three times. (*6 sts*)
Starting with a k row, work 2 rows in st st.
Row 21: [K2tog] three times. (*3 sts*)
Row 22: Purl.
Thread yarn through rem sts to fasten off, leaving length of yarn for sewing up.

Outer ear
(make two)
Using US 2 or 3 (3mm) needles and B, cast on 6 sts. Starting with a k row, work 4 rows in st st.
Row 5: K2, k2tog, k2. (*5 sts*)
Row 6: Purl.
Row 7: Ssk, k1, k2tog. (*3 sts*)
Row 8: CDD. (*1 st*)
Thread yarn through rem st to fasten off.

Inner ear
(make two)
Using US 2 or 3 (3mm) needles and C, cast on 4 sts.
Starting with a k row, work 4 rows in st st.
Row 5: Ssk, k2tog. (*2 sts*)
Row 6: Purl.
Thread yarn through rem sts, leaving length of yarn for sewing up.

savannas, grasslands, and deserts

Mane

Using US 2 or 3 (3mm) needles and A, cast on 7 sts.
Note: When working slipped stitch, always slip sts purlwise to avoid twisting sts.
Row 1: K3, sl1, k3.
Row 2: Purl.
Change to B.
Row 3: K3, sl1, k3.
Row 4: Purl.
Rep last 4 rows six more times.
Change to A.
Row 31: K3, sl1, k3.
Row 32: Purl.
Bind (cast) off.

Making up

Push the safety eyes through the knitting of the head, using the photos as a guide for position. When you are happy with their placement, firmly push the back onto the post of each eye. Using A and starting at the nose, sew the nose seam underneath the head. Change to B and sew the neck closed, skipping the A rows so that the neck curves. Stuff with toy filling.

Using B and starting at the top, sew the seam closed at the front of the body and then continue sewing the seam underneath. Stuff with toy filling. Using the photos for guidance, pin the neck in place ensuring there is enough toy filling inside. Sew the under tail seam of the body, folding the seam to form an upside down T shape. When you are happy with the placement of the neck and head, sew firmly in place.

Using matching yarn, sew the seam along the leg, changing color to sew the foot together. Stuff the foot with toy filling and add a small amount to the leg. Sew the seam at the top of the leg closed. Repeat for the remaining three legs. Pin the legs to the body, using the photos as a guide for position, and then sew in place, with seams facing toward the rear.

Pin an outer ear and an inner ear with WS together. Sew the inner ear in place and then sew the bottom corners of the ear together. Repeat for the second ear. Pin the ears in place, leaving enough space between them for the mane. When you are happy with their placement, sew in place.

Pin the mane in place, using the photos as a guide for position. Sew the mane to the head and neck.

Starting at the end of the tail, sew the side seam of the tail and place a small amount of toy filling inside the end. Pin the tail in place on the back of the body and then sew in place.

TIP Although this pattern includes colorwork, the color changes are on even rows, so you can just carry the non-working yarn up the side of your knitting ready for the next color change.

ziggy the zebra

noodle the giraffe

Skill Level ★★★

This giraffe's neck, body, and legs are knitted using the Fair Isle technique (see page 142), following a chart for each part. The chart will look the same as your knitting, so it's a really clear way to knit colorwork.

Yarn and materials
Rico Ricorumi DK (100% cotton) light worsted (DK) weight yarn, 63yd (58m) per ⅞oz (25g) ball
- 1 ball of Ecru 054 (MC)
- 1 ball of Caramel 053 (light brown) (CC)

Pair of 5mm black domed safety eyes
Toy stuffing

Needles and equipment
US 2 or 3 (3mm) knitting needles
Spare knitting needle for three-needle bind (cast) off
US 2 or 3 (3mm) double-pointed knitting needles for i-cord technique (DPNs)

Stitch markers
Yarn needle
Scissors
Pins

Finished size
Nose to tip of tail: 9½in (24cm)
Foot to top of head (excl ears): 9in (23cm)

Gauge (tension)
Approx 26 sts to 10cm (4in) measured over stockinette (stocking) stitch using US 2 or 3 (3mm) knitting needles.

Abbreviations
See page 143.

Body
Start at front.
Using MC, cast on 29 sts.
Starting with a k row, work 2 rows in st st.
Row 3: K2, M1, k to last 2 sts, M1, k2. (*31 sts*)
Row 4: Purl.
Joining in CC and shaping as indicated, follow Body Chart for 30 rows. (*39 sts*)
Break off CC and cont in MC.
Row 35: K2, ssk, k12, ssk, k3, k2tog, k12, k2tog, k2. (*35 sts*)
Row 36: Purl.
Row 37: K15, ssk, k1, k2tog, k15. (*33 sts*)
Row 38: Purl.

BODY CHART

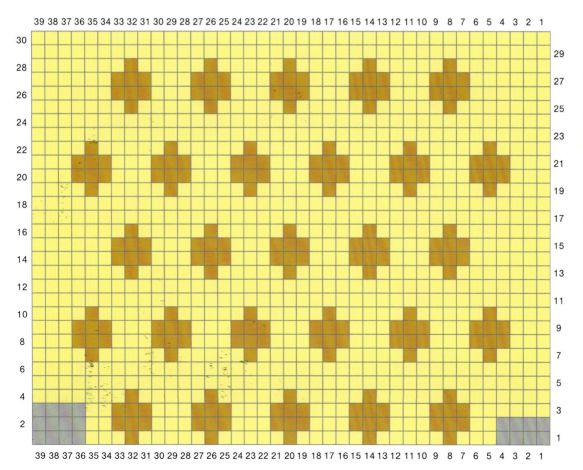

KEY
- RS: knit / WS: purl
- MC
- Gray: no stitch
- CC

Each square represents one stitch. Work odd-number (knit) rows from right to left and even-number (purl) rows from left to right.

Divide rem sts between two needles, 16 sts on one and 17 sts on other. With RS tog and using third needle, bind (cast) off using three-needle bind (cast) off technique (see page 139) to last st, k1 and bind (cast) off.

Head
Using CC, cast on 10 sts.
Row 1 (WS): Purl.
Row 2: K1, M1, k3, M1, k2, M1, k3, M1, k1. (*14 sts*)
Row 3: Purl.
Rep last 2 rows once more. (*18 sts*)
Break off CC and join in MC.
Starting with a k row, work 6 rows in st st.
Row 12: K2, M1, k5, M1, k4, M1, k5, M1, k2. (*22 sts*)
Starting with a p row, work 9 rows in st st.
Row 22: K2, ssk, k4, ssk, k2, k2tog, k4, k2tog, k2. (*18 sts*)
Row 23: Purl.
Row 24: K2, ssk, k2, ssk, k2, k2tog, k2, k2tog, k2. (*14 sts*)
Row 25: Purl.

Divide rem sts evenly between two needles and, with RS tog and using third needle, bind (cast) off using three-needle bind (cast) off technique.

Neck
Using MC yarn, cast on 17 sts.
Joining in CC yarn and increasing as indicated, follow Neck Chart for 20 rows. (*23 sts*)
Bind (cast) off.

Outer ear
(make 2)
Using MC yarn, cast on 5 sts.
Starting with a k row, work 4 rows in st st.
Row 5: K1, CDD, k1. (*3 sts*)
Row 6: CDD. (*1 st*)
Thread yarn through rem st to fasten off.

Inner ear
(make 2)
Using MC yarn, cast on 3 sts.
Starting with a k row, work 5 rows in st st.
Row 6: CDD. (*1 st*)
Thread yarn through rem st to fasten off.

Horn
(make two)
Using CC and DPNs, cast on 3 sts.
Row 1: K3, push sts to other end of needle, pulling yarn firmly across back of work, without turning.
Rep Row 1 three more times.
Turn work.
Beg working flat.
Row 5: [P1, M1] twice, p1. (*5 sts*)
Starting with a k row, work 4 rows in st st.
Row 10: Ssk, k1, k2tog. (*3 sts*)
Thread yarn through rem sts, leaving length of yarn for sewing up.

Leg and foot
(make 4)
Using MC, cast on 13 sts.
Joining in CC yarn as indicated, beg with a p row, follow Leg Chart for 18 rows.
Break off MC and cont in CC:
Row 19: Purl.
Row 20: K5, M1, k3, M1, k5. (*15 sts*)
Row 21: P6, M1, p3, M1, p6. (*17 sts*)
Row 22: K7, M1, k3, M1, k7. (*19 sts*)

NECK CHART

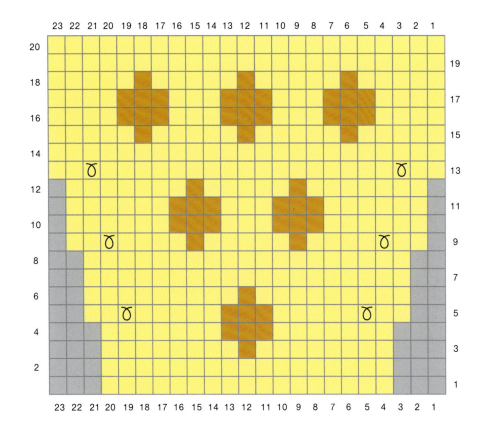

KEY

- RS: knit / WS: purl
- MC
- Gray: no stitch
- CC
- RS: M1

Each square represents one stitch. Work odd-number (knit) rows from right to left and even-number (purl) rows from left to right.

26 savannas, grasslands, and deserts

LEG CHART

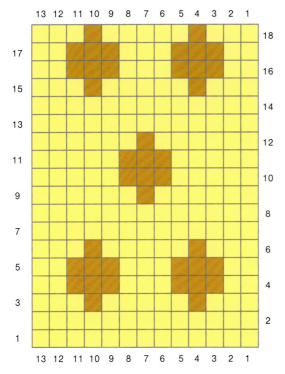

KEY

☐ RS: knit / WS: purl
▨ MC
▨ CC

Each square represents one stitch. Work odd-number (purl) rows from left to right and even-number (knit) rows from right to left.

Making up

Using matching yarn, sew the seam on the body that will be underneath, stuffing with toy filling as you go. Sew the front seam of the body, folding the seam to form an upside down T shape. Sew the seam along the back of the neck, stuff with toy filling, and pin to the body using the photos as a guide for position. Sew in place.

Stuff the head slightly and pin together. Push the safety eyes through the knitting and when you are happy with their placement, remove the pins and toy filling and firmly push the back onto the post of each eye. Re-stuff the head and, using matching yarn, sew the seam underneath the head and nose. Pin the head to the top of the neck, using the photos for guidance. Sew in place.

With an inner and outer ear WS together, sew the lining inside the ear. Repeat for second ear and then pin both ears in place on the top of the head, leaving enough space in between for the horns. Sew in place. Gather the top of the horn and sew together. Place the horns in between the ears and sew in place.

Using matching yarn, sew the foot seam. Stuff the foot with toy filling, but do not add toy filling to the leg. Sew the leg seam closed and sew the seam at the top of the leg so that the top of the side seam is facing toward the back of the leg. Repeat for the other three legs. Using the photos as a guide, pin each leg in place to the body. Sew in place.

To make the fluffy end of the tail, thread a yarn needle with a double length of MC and sew from the base of the tail up inside, leave about 1in (2.5cm) hanging, then thread the needle back down so that there are now eight strands of yarn at the bottom of the tail plus the bound- (cast-) off length. Separate out the ply of each piece of yarn and trim to length. Sew the tail to the body.

Starting with a p row, work 3 rows in st st.
Row 26: K6, ssk, k3, k2tog, k6. (*17 sts*)
Row 27: Purl.
Row 28: K1, ssk, k2, ssk, k3, k2tog, k2, k2tog, k1. (*13 sts*)
Row 29: Purl.
Divide rem sts between two needles, 6 sts on one and 7 sts on other. With RS tog and using third needle, bind (cast) off using three-needle bind (cast) off technique to last st, k1 and bind (cast) off.

Tail

Using MC and DPNs, cast on 4 sts.
Row 1: K4, push sts to other end of needle, pulling yarn firmly across back of work, without turning.
Rep Row 1 nine more times.
Thread yarn through rem sts to fasten off.

noodle the giraffe 27

tank the tortoise

Skill Level ★★★

The tortoise's shell is knitted using blocks of stockinette (stocking) stitch and reverse stockinette stitch to create the markings. A tortoise called Jonathan is one of the longest-living land animals in the world, at over 190 years old!

Yarn and materials
Rico Ricorumi DK (100% cotton) light worsted (DK) weight yarn, 63yd (58m) per ⅞oz (25g) ball
  1 ball each of:
    Nougat 056 (light brown) (MC)
    Olive 048 (green) (CC)
Small amount of black fingering (4-ply) weight yarn (A)
Toy filling
Pair of 5mm black domed safety eyes

Needles and equipment
US 2 or 3 (3mm) knitting needles
Crochet hook
Spare knitting needle for three-needle bind (cast) off
Yarn needle
Scissors
Pins

Finished size
Nose to tail: approx 2¼in (5.5cm)

Gauge (tension)
Approx 26 sts to 4in (10cm) measured over stockinette (stocking) stitch using US 2 or 3 (3mm) knitting needles.

Abbreviations
See page 143.

Top of shell

Cast on using applied i-cord technique (see page 134) as foll:
Using MC, cast on 3 sts.

I-cord row 1: K3, push sts to other end of needle, pulling yarn firmly across back of work, without turning.

Rep i-cord row 1 seventy more times. Slide the three stitches to the end of your needle and knit them together.

Use a crochet hook to pick up 70 sts along row edge of i-cord. (71 sts)

Row 1: [K5, p2] 9 times, k5, p3.

Slip stitches purlwise with yarn on WS.

Row 2 (RS): P1, sl2, [p5, sl2] 9 times, p5.

Row 3: [K5, p2] 9 times, k5, p3.

Rep last 2 rows twice more.

Row 8: P1, [sl2, p5] 9 times, sl2, p5.

Row 9: P5, [p2tog, p5] 9 times, p2tog, p1. (*61 sts*)

Row 10: Knit.

Row 11: K2, [p2, k4] 9 times, p2, k3.

Row 12: P3, [sl2, p4] 9 times, sl2, p2.

Rep last 2 rows once more.

Row 15: K2, [p2, k4] 9 times, p2, k3.

Row 16: K2tog, k1, [k2tog, k1, k2tog, k1] 9 times, [k2tog] twice. (*40 sts*)

Row 17: P1, p2tog, [p2, p2tog] 9 times, p1. (*30 sts*)

Row 18: [Sl1, p2] 10 times.

Row 19: [K2, p1] 10 times.

Rep last 2 rows once more.

Row 22: [Sl1, p2] 10 times.

Row 23: [P2tog, p11, p2togtbl] twice. (*26 sts*)

Divide rem sts evenly between two needles and, with RS tog and using third needle, bind (cast) off using three-needle bind (cast) off technique (see page 139).

Base

Using CC, cast on 8 sts.

Row 1 (WS): Purl.

Row 2: K1, M1, k to last st, M1, k1. (*10 sts*)

Row 3: Purl.

Rep last 2 rows once more. (*12 sts*)

Row 6: K1, M1, k to last st, M1, k1. (*14 sts*)

Row 7: P1, M1, p to last st, M1, p1. (*16 sts*)

Rep last 2 rows once more. (*20 sts*)

Row 10: K1, M1, k to last st, M1, k1. (*22 sts*)

Starting with a p row, work 11 rows in st st.

Row 22: K1, ssk, k to last 3 sts, k2tog, k1. (*20 sts*)

Row 23: Purl.

Row 24: K1, ssk, k to last 3 sts, k2tog, k1. (*18 sts*)

Row 25: P1, p2tog, p to last 3 sts, p2togtbl, p1. (*16 sts*)

Row 26: K1, ssk, k to last 3 sts, k2tog, k1. (*14 sts*)

Row 27: Purl.

Rep last 4 rows once more. (*8 sts*)

Bind (cast) off.

Head

Using CC, cast on 14 sts.

Starting with a k row, work 2 rows in st st.

Row 3: K5, M1, k4, M1, k5. (*16 sts*)

Row 4: Purl.

Row 5: K6, M1, k4, M1, k6. (*18 sts*)

Row 6: Purl.

Row 7: K7, M1, k4, M1, k7. (*20 sts*)

Starting with a p row, work 5 rows in st st.

Row 13: K2, ssk, k2, ssk, k4, k2tog, k2, k2tog, k2. (*16 sts*)

Row 14: Purl.

Row 15: K2, ssk, ssk, k4, k2tog, k2tog, k2. (*12 sts*)

Row 16: Purl.

Bind (cast) off.

Leg

(make 4)

Using CC, cast on 8 sts.

Starting with a k row, work 6 rows in st st.

Row 7: K3, M1, k2, M1, k3. (*10 sts*)

Row 8: P4, M1, p2, M1, p4. (*12 sts*)

Row 9: Knit.

Row 10: Purl.

Row 11: K3, ssk, k2, k2tog, k3. (*10 sts*)

Row 12: P2, p2tog, p2, p2togtbl, p2. (*8 sts*)

Row 13: K1, ssk, k2, k2tog, k1. (*6 sts*)

Thread yarn through rem sts and fasten off.

Tail

Using CC, cast on 12 sts.

Starting with a k row, work 2 rows in st st.

Row 3: K2, ssk, k4, k2tog, k2. (*10 sts*)

Row 4: Purl.

Row 5: K2, ssk, k2, k2tog, k2. (*8 sts*)

Row 6: P1, p2tog, p2, p2togtbl, p1. (*6 sts*)

Row 7: K1, ssk, k2tog, k1. (*4 sts*)

Row 8: P2tog, p2togtbl. (*2 sts*)

Thread yarn through rem sts to fasten off.

Making up

Pin the head together and stuff with toy filling. Add the safety eyes to the head by pushing through the knitting using the photos as a guide for position. When you are happy with the placement, remove the pins and toy filling and firmly push the backs onto the post of each eye.

Starting at the top of the head, sew the seam to the base of the body, stuffing with toy filling as you go. Sew the cast-on edge closed with the side seam of the head in the middle of the seam forming a T shape.

Sew the side seam of the leg and stuff the foot with toy filling. The side seam will be underneath the leg. Using the photos as a guide for position, pin each leg, the head, and the tail to the shell—you can stuff the shell to help with this. Sew in place, stitching just inside the cast-on edge of the shell.

Pin the base in place then sew, stuffing with toy filling as you go.

Embroider the mouth using A and backstitch (see page 142).

Skill Level ★ ★ ★

growly the lion

Did you know that because male lions are larger, they are less likely to be successful hunters than female lions? This friendly lion is knitted using the same fluffy yarn as the orangutan on page 39. The mane and end of the tail are knitted in reverse stockinette (stocking) stitch, so the fluffiest part of the yarn is on the outside.

Yarn and materials

Rico Ricorumi DK (100% cotton) light worsted (DK) weight yarn, 63yd (58m) per ⅞oz (25g) ball

    2 balls of Sand 071 (yellow) (MC)

    Small amount of Chocolate 057 (dark brown) (CC1)

King Cole Moments DK (100% polyester) light worsted (DK) weight yarn, 98yd (90m) per 1¾oz (50g) ball

    1 ball of Ginger 1876 (orange) (CC2)

Pair of 5mm black domed safety eyes

Needles and equipment

US 2 or 3 (3mm) knitting needles

Spare knitting needles

Yarn needle

Scissors

Pins

Finished size

Top of head to toe: 9½in (24cm)

Gauge (tension)

Approx 26 sts to 4in (10cm) measured over stockinette (stocking) stitch using US 2 or 3 (3mm) knitting needles.

Abbreviations

See page 143.

Head

Start at nose.

Using CC1, cast on 3 sts.

Row 1 (WS): Purl.

Row 2: [K1, M1] twice, k1. (5 *sts*)

Row 3: Purl.

Rep last 2 rows once more. (7 *sts*)

Row 6: Knit.

Row 7: Purl.

Break yarn and leave sts on a spare needle.

Muzzle

SIDE 1

Using MC, cast on 7 sts.

Row 1: Purl.

Row 2: K to last st, M1, k1. (8 *sts*)

Row 3: Purl.

Rep last 2 rows once more. (9 *sts*)

Break yarn and leave sts on a spare needle.

SIDE 2

Using MC, cast on 7 sts.

Row 1: Purl.

Row 2: K1, M1, k to end. (8 *sts*)

Row 3: Purl.

Rep last 2 rows once more. (9 *sts*)

Row 6: Using MC, k9, with RS facing, k across 7 held nose sts, with RS facing, k across side 1 of muzzle. (25 *sts*)

Row 7: Purl.

Row 8: Knit.

Row 9: Purl.

Row 10: K3, M1, k5, M1, k9, M1, k5, M1, k3. (29 *sts*)

Row 11: Purl.

Shaping is done with short rows (see page 140).

Row 12: K9, turn.

Row 13: Slds, p5, turn.

Row 14: Slds, k22, turn.

Row 15: Slds, p5, turn.

Row 16: Slds, k to end.

Row 17: Purl.

30   *savannas, grasslands, and deserts*

Chapter 2
forests and jungles

rainbow the chameleon

Skill Level ★★★

The color-changing yarn used for this cute chameleon really enhances the design. The tail is knitted using the i-cord technique and the spine is also an i-cord which you sew on.

Yarn and materials

Ricorumi Print DK (100% cotton) light worsted (DK) weight yarn, 62yd (57.5m) per ⅞oz (25g) ball

  1¼ balls of Green Mix 005 (MC)

Small amount of black fingering (4-ply) weight yarn

Pair of 5mm black domed safety eyes

Toy filling

Needles and equipment

US 2 or 3 (3mm) knitting needles

Pair of US 2 or 3 (3mm) double-pointed needles (DPNs)

Stitch markers

Yarn needle

Scissors

Pins

Finished size

Tail to nose 7½in (19cm)

Foot to top of crest 4in (10cm)

Gauge (tension)

Approx 26 sts to 4in (10cm) measured over stockinette (stocking) stitch using US 2 or 3 (3mm) knitting needles.

Abbreviations

See page 143.

Tail, body, and head

Start at end of tail.
Using MC, cast on 4 sts.
Starting with a k row, work 2 rows in st st.
Shaping is done with short rows (see page 140).
Row 3: K3, turn.
Row 4: Slds, p1, turn.
Row 5: Slds, k to end.
Row 6: Purl.
Rep Rows 3–6 once more.
Row 11: K1, M1, k2, M1, k1. (*6 sts*)
Row 12: Purl.
Row 13: K5, turn.
Row 14: Slds, p3, turn.
Row 15: Slds, k to end.
Row 16: Purl.
Rep Rows 13–16 six more times.
Row 41: K1, M1, k to last st, M1, k1. (*8 sts*)
Row 42: Purl.
Row 43: K7, turn.
Row 44: Slds, p5, turn.
Row 45: Slds, k to end.
Starting with a p row, work 3 rows in st st.
Row 49: K7, turn.
Row 50: Slds, p5, turn.
Row 51: Slds, k to end.
Row 52: Purl.
Row 53: K1, M1, k to last st, M1, k1. (*10 sts*)
Row 54: Purl.
Row 55: K9, turn.
Row 56: Slds, p7, turn.
Row 57: Slds, k to end.
Row 58: Purl.
Row 59: K1, M1, k3, M1, k2, M1, k3, M1, k1. (*14 sts*)
Row 60: Purl.
Row 61: K1, [M1, k2] 6 times, M1, k1. (*21 sts*)
Row 62: Purl.
Row 63: K1, M1, [k2, M1] 4 times, k3, [M1, k2] 4 times, M1, k1. (*31 sts*)
Starting with a p row, work 3 rows in st st.
Row 67: K2, [M1, k4] 3 times, M1, k3, [M1, k4] 3 times, M1, k2. (*39 sts*)
PM either side of 3 center sts (leaving 18 sts each side).
Row 68: Purl, slipping markers.

Row 69: K to marker, M1, SM, k to marker, SM, M1, k to end. (*41 sts*)
Starting with a p row, work 3 rows in st st, SM on each row.
Rep last 4 rows once more. (*43 sts*)
Starting with a k row, work 4 rows in st st.
Row 81: K to 2 sts before marker, k2tog, SM, k to marker, SM, ssk, k to end. (*41 sts*)
Starting with a p row, work 3 rows in st st.
Rep last 4 rows once more. (*39 sts*)
Remove markers.
Row 89: [K4, k2tog] 3 times, k3, [ssk, k4] 3 times. (*33 sts*)
Starting with a p row, work 3 rows in reverse st st.
Row 93: K15, k2tog. (*16 sts*)
Leave rem 16 sts on spare knitting needle.
Work first side of head as foll:
Row 94: Cast on 5 sts, p to end. (*21 sts*)
Starting with a k row, work 2 rows in st st.
Row 97: K to last 3 sts, k2tog, k1. (*20 sts*)
Row 98: Purl.
Rep Rows 97 and 98 twice more. (*18 sts*)
Row 103: K to last 3 sts, k2tog, k1. (*17 sts*)
Break yarn. Leave sts on spare needle.
Work second side of head as foll:
With WS facing, rejoin yarn to rem 16 sts.
Row 93: Purl.
Row 94: Cast on 5 sts, k to end. (*21 sts*)
Starting with a p row, work 2 rows in st st.
Row 97: P to last 3 sts, p2tog, p1. (*20 sts*)
Row 98: Knit.
Rep Rows 97 and 98 twice more. (*18 sts*)
Row 103: P to last 3 sts, p2tog, p1. (*17 sts*)
Break yarn.
With WS facing, place both sides of head back on same needle, with cast-on sts for crest in middle. (*34 sts*)
Rejoin yarn and purl 1 row.
Next row: K1, k2tog, k to last 3 sts, ssk, k1. (*32 sts*)
Next row: P13, p2togtbl, p2, p2tog, p13. (*30 sts*)
Next row: K1, k2tog, k to last 3 sts, ssk, k1. (*28 sts*)
Next row: P11, p2togtbl, p2, p2tog, p11. (*26 sts*)
Next row: K1, k2tog, k7, k2tog, k2, ssk, k7, ssk, k1. (*22 sts*)
Next row: P8, p2togtbl, p2, p2tog, p8. (*20 sts*)
Divide rem sts evenly between two needles and, with RS tog and using a DPN, bind (cast) off using three-needle bind (cast) off technique (see page 139).

rainbow the chameleon   37

Eye

(make two)
Using MC, cast on 12 sts.
Row 1 (WS): Purl.
Shaping is done with short rows.
Row 2: K8, turn.
Row 3: Slds, p3, turn.
Row 4: Slds, k to end.
Row 5: Purl.
Row 6: [K2tog] 6 times. (*6 sts*)
Thread yarn through rem sts to gather, leaving a length of yarn for sewing up.

Foot and leg

(make four)
Foot is worked in two halves then joined to make leg.
*Using MC, cast on 4 sts.
Starting with a k row, work 2 rows in st st.
Row 3: K1, k2tog, k1. (*3 sts*)
Starting with a p row, work 9 rows in st st.
Row 13: K1, M1, k2. (*4 sts*)
Row 14: Purl.
Row 15: K1, M1, k2, M1, k1. (*6 sts*)
Break yarn. Place sts on spare needle.*
Work from * to * once more.
Place both sets of sts with WS facing on one needle for beg of leg.
Row 16: Purl. (*12 sts*)
Starting with a k row, work 4 rows in st st.
Cont in st st, bind (cast) off 2 sts at beg of next 2 rows. (*8 sts*)
Row 23: K1, ssk, k to last 3 sts, k1. (*6 sts*)
Row 24: Purl.
Rep Rows 23 and 24 once more. (*4 sts*)
Bind (cast) off.

Crest for back

Using DPNs and MC, cast on 3 sts.
Row 1: K3, push sts to other end of needle, pulling yarn firmly across back of work, without turning.
Rep Row 1 until piece is four rows shorter than length of back of body, using photo as a guide.
Next row: K2tog, k1. (*2 sts*)
Cont in st st for 3 rows.
Thread yarn through rem sts to fasten, leaving length of yarn for sewing up.

Making up

Sew the side seam on the eye. Push the safety eye through the middle of the gathered bound- (cast-) off edge and firmly push the backs onto the post of each eye. Place a small amount of toy filling inside the eye. Repeat for second eye.

Starting at the end of the tail, sew the tail seam together, pushing a tiny amount of toy filling inside and pulling the yarn slightly tighter to help the tail curl round. Continue sewing the seam along the bottom edge of the body and head, stuffing with toy filling as you go. Sew the head closed at the chin. Sew the edge of the tail to the underneath of the base of the body to keep the tail in place. Sew the crest seam on the chameleon's head together, adding toy filling as necessary. Sew the back crest in place by catching a stitch underneath the crest and sewing to the back, repeating along the length.

Using the photos for guidance, pin the eyes in place on each side of the head so that the deeper section of the eye is facing outward. This will help the eyes look forward. When you are happy with their placement, sew in place.

With RS together, sew the two cast-on edges of the foot together, then sew the side seam of the leg from the top to the bottom. Fold the foot section in half so the cast-on seam is in the center of the underfoot. Sew the seam of the foot on one side from fold to fold to create toes. Sew other side. Stuff with toy filling, adding a small amount to each "toe" to add definition. Repeat for the other three legs and feet. Pin each leg and foot in place using the photos as a guide for position, and when you are happy with their placement, sew firmly in place.

Embroider the mouth on the front of the face using A and backstitch (see page 142).

38 forests and jungles

huggy the orangutan

This little orangutan is knitted using an amazing fluffy yarn. I discovered that the wrong side of the work (purl) is fluffier than the right side, so all the fluffy parts are worked using reverse stockinette (stocking) stitch. When you sew your orangutan up you can use the plain yarn to make it easier to see.

Skill Level ★★★

Yarn and materials
King Cole Moments DK (100% polyester) light worsted (DK) weight yarn, 98yd (90m) per 1¾oz (50g) ball
- 1 ball of Ginger 1876 (orange) (MC)

Rico Ricorumi DK (100% cotton) light worsted (DK) weight yarn, 63yd (58m) per ⅞oz (25g) ball
- ⅓ ball of Caramel 053 (light brown) (CC)

Small amount of black light worsted (DK) weight yarn (A)

Toy filling
Pair of 5mm black domed safety eyes

Needles and equipment
US 2 or 3 (3mm) knitting needles
Spare knitting needle
Stitch markers
Yarn needle
Scissors
Pins

Finished size
Base to top of head: 4¼in (11cm)

Gauge (tension)
Approx 26 sts to 4in (10cm) measured over stockinette (stocking) stitch using US 2 or 3 (3mm) knitting needles and light worsted (DK) weight yarn.

Abbreviations
See page 143.

Pattern note
When using the MC, working in reverse st st means the fluffier side is on show.

Nose
Using CC, cast on 5 sts.
Row 1 (RS): K1, M1, k to last st, M1, k1. (*7 sts*)
Row 2: P1, M1, p to last st, M1, p1. (*9 sts*)
Shaping is done with short rows (see page 140).
Row 3: K7, turn.
Row 4: Slds, p4, turn.
Row 5: Slds, k to end.
Row 6: Purl.
Row 7: K7, turn.
Row 8: Slds, p4, turn.
Row 9: Slds, k3, turn.
Row 10: Slds, p2, turn.
Row 11: Slds, k to end.
Row 12: Purl.
Row 13: K1, ssk, k3, k2tog, k1. (*7 sts*)
Row 14: P1, p2tog, p1, p2togtbl, p1. (*5 sts*)
Cut yarn and leave on spare needle.

Head and body
Using MC, cast on 11 sts.
Work in reverse st st.
Row 1 (RS): Purl.
Row 2: K1, M1, k to last st, M1, k1. (*13 sts*)
Row 3: Purl.
Row 4: K1, M1, k4, M1, k3, M1, k4, M1, k1. (*17 sts*)
Row 5: Purl.
Row 6: K7, M1, k3, M1, k7. (*19 sts*)

huggy the orangutan 39

Starting with a p row, work 7 rows in st st.
Row 14: K1, ssk, k to last 3 sts, k2tog, k1. (*17 sts*)
Row 15: P1, p2tog, p to last 3 sts, p2togtbl, p1. (*15 sts*)
Change to CC yarn.
Row 16: Purl.
Join in nose section
Row 17: K5, with nose section in front of face and RS facing toward you, k next st on needle tog with first st on spare needle, rep four more times (nose section will now be joined), k5. (*15 sts*)

Starting with a p row, work 3 rows in st st.
Row 21: K1, ssk, k to last 3 sts, k2tog, k1. (*13 sts*)
Row 22: P1, p2togtbl, p to last 3 sts, p2tog, p1. (*11 sts*)
Rep last 2 rows once more. (*7 sts*)
Change to MC.
Row 25: Knit.
Cont in reverse st st.
Row 26 (WS): K1, M1, k2, M1, k1, M1, k2, M1, k1. (*11 sts*)
Row 27: Purl.
Row 28: K1, M1, k3, M1, k3, M1, k3, M1, k1. (*15 sts*)

40 **forests and jungles**

Row 29: Purl.
Row 30: K1, M1, k5, M1, k3, M1, k5, M1, k1. (*19 sts*)
Row 31: Purl.
Row 32: K1, M1, k7, M1, k3, M1, k7, M1, k1. (*23 sts*)
Row 33: Purl.
Row 34: K1, M1, k9, M1, k3, M1, k9, M1, k1. (*27 sts*)
Starting with a p row, work 15 rows in st st.
Row 50: K1, M1, k11, M1, k3, M1, k11, M1, k1. (*31 sts*)
Starting with a p row, work 11 rows in st st.
PM either side of center 13 sts, leaving 9 sts on each side.
Row 62: K to 2 sts before marker, ssk, SM, k to marker, SM, k2tog, k to end. (*29 sts*)
Row 63: Purl.
Rep last 2 rows 7 more times. (*15 sts*)
Remove markers.
Row 78: K1, M1, k to last st, M1, k1. (*17 sts*)
Row 79: P1, M1, p to last st, M1, p1. (*19 sts*)
Starting with a k row, work 8 rows in st st.
Row 88: K1, ssk, k to last 3 sts, k2tog, k1. (*17 sts*)
Row 89: Purl.
Rep last 2 rows 3 more times. (*11 sts*)
Bind (cast) off.

Right arm/leg
(make two)
*Using MC, cast on 6 sts.
Work in reverse st st.
Row 1 (RS): Purl.
Row 2: K1, M1, k to last st, M1, k1. (*8 sts*)
Row 3: Purl.
Rep last 2 rows twice more. (*12 sts*)
Shaping is done with short rows.
Row 8: K10, turn.
Row 9: Slds, p7, turn.
Row 10: Slds, k5, turn.
Row 11: Slds, p3, turn.
Row 12: Slds, k to end.
Starting with a p row, work 15 rows in st st.
Change to CC.
Starting with a p row, work 3 rows in st st.*
Now beg working thumb at edge of row only.
Row 31: K to end of row and, wyib sl last 3 sts from RH needle to LH needle.
Row 32: Do not turn, pull yarn across back of work, k3, wyib sl3 sts from RH needle to LH needle.
Row 33: Do not turn, pull yarn across back of work, k3.
Thread yarn through sts and fasten off, leaving length of yarn for sewing up.
With WS facing, rejoin CC to next st on needle, p to end. (*9 sts*)
Next row: Knit.
Next row: Purl.
Next row: [K1, k2tog] twice, k2tog, k1. (*6 sts*)
Thread yarn through rem sts to fasten off, leaving length of yarn for sewing up.

Left arm/leg
(make two)
As right arm/leg from * to *.
Now beg working thumb at edge of row only.
Row 31: K3, wyib sl sts from RH needle to LH needle.
Row 32: Do not turn, pull yarn across back of work, k3, wyib sl3 sts from RH needle to LH needle.
Row 33: Do not turn, pull yarn across back of work, k3.
Thread yarn through sts and fasten off, leaving length of yarn for sewing up.
With RS facing, rejoin CC to next st on needle, k to end. (*9 sts*)
Starting with a p row, work 2 rows in st st.
Next row: [P1, p2tog] twice, p2tog, k1. (*6 sts*)
Thread yarn through rem sts to fasten off, leaving length of yarn for sewing up.

Making up
Being a smooth yarn it may be easier to make up using CC.

Push the safety eyes through the knitting 3 rows above the joining of the nose section, with 3 sts between them, using the photos for guidance. When you are happy with their placement, firmly push the backs on.

Starting at the top of the head, sew along one of the side seams, matching the front of the head to the back. Stuff the head with toy filling and sew the second side seam, adding more toy filling as needed.

Fold the front of the body up so that the shaped base is at the bottom. The front of the head will overlap the body. Sew one side seam closed, stuff with toy filling and sew the second side seam closed. Making sure there is enough toy filling inside the head and body, sew the bottom of the head to the body, adding more toy filling as you go. Sew the nose section to the front of the head, stuffing with toy filling.

Sew the side seam of the arm/leg, which will be facing the body when you sew the arms and legs on. Stuff with toy filling as you go. Sew the hand and thumb together, stuffing the hand with toy filling. Repeat for the three other limbs. Pin the arms and legs to the body using the photos as a guide for position. Sew firmly to the body.

Using A, embroider the nose using two chain stitches and the mouth using backstitch (see page 142).

Skill Level ★ ★ ★

honey the sun bear

What gives this sweet bear so much character is his little eyebrows. They are made while you knit the head with a small amount of short-row shaping so there's nothing to sew on later!

Yarn and materials

Rowan Felted Tweed (50% wool, 25% viscose, 25% alpaca) light worsted (DK) weight yarn, 191yd (175m) per 1¾oz (50g) ball

- ¾ ball of Phantom 153 (dark brown) (MC)
- ¼ ball of Cinnamon 175 (light brown) (CC)

Small amount of black fingering (4-ply) yarn (A)

Pair of 6mm black domed safety eyes

Toy filling

Needles and equipment

US 2 or 3 (3mm) knitting needles

Spare knitting needle for three-needle bind (cast) off

Yarn needle

Scissors

Pins

Finished size

Base to top of head: 7½in (19cm)

Gauge (tension)

Approx 26 sts to 4in (10cm) measured over stockinette (stocking) stitch using US 2 or 3 (3mm) knitting needles.

Abbreviations

See page 143.

Head

Start at nose.

Using CC, cast on 12 sts.

Row 1 (WS): Purl.

Row 2: K1, M1, k to last st, M1, k1. (*14 sts*)

Row 3: P1, M1, p to last st, M1, p1. (*16 sts*)

Rep Rows 2 and 3 once more. (*20 sts*)

Row 6: K1, M1, k to last st, M1, k1. (*22 sts*)

Row 7: Purl.

Bind (cast) off.

With RS facing and using MC, pick up and k 22 sts from bound- (cast-) off edge, then p 1 row.

Row 1: K4, M1, [k2, M1] 3 times, k2, [M1, k2] 3 times, M1, k4. (*30 sts*)

Row 2: Purl.

Shaping is done with short rows (see page 140).

Row 3: K13, turn.

Row 4: Slds, p4, turn.

Row 5: Slds, k3, turn.

Row 6: Slds, p2, turn.

Row 7: Slds, k11, turn.

Row 8: Slds, p4, turn.

Row 9: Slds, k3, turn.

Row 10: Slds, p2, turn.

Row 11: Slds, k to end.

This short row shaping forms eyebrows.

Row 12: P8, *put needle through next st purlwise and pick up st directly underneath st 3 rows down and p1 through loops; rep from * four more times** (this will form the eyebrow), p4, work from * to ** again to complete second eyebrow, p to end.

TIP There is just a small amount of short row shaping in this pattern, so if you haven't tried it before, this would be a good project to start with.

42 **forests and jungles**

Row 13: K5, [M1, k5] 4 times, M1, k5. (*35 sts*)
Starting with a p row, work 3 rows in st st.
Row 17: [K6, M1] 5 times, k5. (*40 sts*)
Row 18: Purl.
Row 19: [K4, M1] 4 times, k3, M1, k2, M1, k3, [M1, k4] 4 times. (*50 sts*)
Starting with a p row, work 5 rows in st st.
Row 25: K4, ssk, [k3, ssk] 3 times, k8, [k2tog, k3] 3 times, k2tog, k4. (*42 sts*)
Row 26: Purl.
Row 27: [K3, ssk] 4 times, k2, [k2tog, k3] 4 times. (*34 sts*)
Row 28: Purl.
Row 29: [K2, ssk] 4 times, k2, [k2tog, k2] 4 times. (*26 sts*)
Row 30: Purl.
Row 31: K3, [k1, ssk] 3 times, k2, [k1, k2tog] 3 times, k3. (*20 sts*)
Row 32: Purl.
Divide rem sts evenly between two needles and, with RS tog and using third needle, bind (cast) off using three-needle bind (cast) off technique (see page 139).

Body
Start at neck.
Using MC, cast on 40 sts.
Rows 1–14: Starting with a k row, work in st st.
Row 15: K9, M1, k2, M1, k18, M1, k2, M1, k9. (*44 sts*)
Starting with a p row, work 3 rows in st st.
Row 19: K10, M1, k2, M1, k20, M1, k2, M1, k10. (*48 sts*)
Starting with a p row, work 3 rows in st st.
Row 23: K23, M1, k2, M1, k23. (*50 sts*)
Row 24: Purl.
Row 25: K23, M1, k4, M1, k23. (*52 sts*)
Row 26: Purl.
Row 27: K23, M1, k6, M1, k23. (*54 sts*)
Starting with a p row, work 9 rows in st st.
Row 37: K10, ssk, k2, k2tog, k22, ssk, k2, k2tog, k10. (*50 sts*)
Row 26: Purl.
Cont working in st st and bind (cast) off 19 sts at beg of next 2 rows. (*12 sts*)
Cont base of body as foll:
Row 29: K2, M1, k to last 2 sts, M1, k2. (*14 sts*)
Row 30: Purl.
Rep Rows 29 and 30 three more times. (*20 sts*)
Starting with a k row, work 8 rows in st st.
Row 45: K2, ssk, k to last 4 sts, k2tog, k2. (*18 sts*)
Row 46: Purl.
Rep Rows 45 and 46 once more. (*16 sts*)
Row 49: K2, ssk, k to last 4 sts, k2tog, k2. (*14 sts*)
Row 50: P2, p2togtbl, p to last 4 sts, p2tog, p2. (*12 sts*)
Bind (cast) off.

Right leg and foot
Using MC, cast on 6 sts.
Row 1 (WS): Purl.
Row 2: K1, M1, k to last st, M1, k1. (*8 sts*)
Row 3: Purl.

Rep Rows 2 and 3 once more. (*10 sts*)
Cast on 1 st at beg of next row, k to end. (*11 sts*)
Cast on 7 sts at beg of next row, p to end. (*18 sts*)
*Starting with a k row, work 4 rows in st st.
Row 12: K8, M1, k2, M1, k8. (*20 sts*)
Row 13: P9, M1, p2, M1, p9. (*22 sts*)
Row 14: K10, M1, k2, M1, k10. (*24 sts*)
Row 15: P11, M1, p2, M1, p11. (*26 sts*)
Row 16: K12, M1, k2, M1, k12. (*28 sts*)
Row 17: P13, M1, p2, M1, p13. (*30 sts*)
Starting with a k row, work 2 rows in st st.
Cont working in st st and bind (cast) off 13 sts at beg of next 2 rows. (*4 sts*)
Row 22: Knit.
Change to CC.
Row 23: P1, M1, p to last st, M1, p1. (*6 sts*)
Row 24: K1, M1, k to last st, M1, k1. (*8 sts*)
Row 25: P1, M1, p to last st, M1, p1. (*10 sts*)
Starting with a k row, work 4 rows in st st.
Row 30: K1, ssk, k4, k2tog, k1. (*8 sts*)
Row 31: P1, p2togtbl, p2, p2tog, p1. (*6 sts*)
Row 32: K1, ssk, k2tog, k1. (*4 sts*)
Row 33: Purl.
Bind (cast) off.
Thread yarn through rem sts to fasten off, leaving length of yarn for sewing up.*

Left leg and foot
Using MC, cast on 6 sts.
Row 1 (WS): Purl.
Row 2: K1, M1, k to last st, M1, k1. (*8 sts*)
Row 3: Purl.
Rep Rows 2 and 3 once more. (*10 sts*)
Cast on 7 sts at beg of next row, k to end. (*17 sts*)
Cast on 1 st at beg of next row, p to end. (*18 sts*)
Work as for left leg and foot from * to *.

Right arm
Using MC, cast on 4 sts.
Row 1 (RS): Knit.
Row 2: P1, M1, p to last st, M1, p1. (*6 sts*)
Row 3: Knit.
Rep Rows 2 and 3 once more. (*8 sts*)
Cast on 8 sts at beg of next row, p to end. (*16 sts*)
Starting with a k row, work 8 rows in st st.
Shaping is done with short rows.
Row 15: K4, turn.
Row 16: Slds, p to end.
Row 17: K3, turn.
Row 18: Slds, p to end.
Row 19: Knit.
Row 20: P4, turn.
Row 21: Slds, k to end.
Row 22: P3, turn.
Row 23: Slds, k to end.
Starting with a p row, work 5 rows in st st.

44 forests and jungles

Join in CC and cont as foll:
Row 29: Using MC, k9, using CC, k7.
Row 30: Using CC, p7, using MC, p9.
Rep Rows 29 and 30 once more.
Row 33: Using MC, k1, ssk, k3, k2tog, k1, using CC, ssk, k3, k2tog. (*12 sts*)
Row 34: Purl, working colors as set.
Row 35: Using MC, k1, ssk, k1, k2tog, k1, using CC, ssk, k1, k2tog. (*8 sts*)
Divide rem sts evenly between two needles and, with RS tog and using third needle, bind (cast) off using three-needle bind (cast) off technique.

Left arm
Using MC, cast on 4 sts.
Row 1 (WS): Purl.
Row 2: K1, M1, k to last st, M1, k1. (*6 sts*)
Row 3: Purl.
Rep Rows 2 and 3 once more. (*8 sts*)
Cast on 8 sts at beg of next row, k to end. (*16 sts*)
Starting with a p row, work 8 rows in st st.
Shaping is done with short rows.
Row 15: P4, turn.
Row 16: Slds, k to end.
Row 17: P3, turn.
Row 18: Slds, k to end.
Row 19: Purl.
Row 20: K4, turn.
Row 21: Slds, p to end.
Row 22: K3, turn.
Row 23: Slds, p to end.
Starting with a k row, work 4 rows in st st.
Join in CC yarn and cont as foll:
Row 28: Using CC, k7, using MC, k9.
Row 29: Using MC, p9, using CC, p7.
Rep Rows 28 and 29 once more.
Row 32: Using CC, ssk, k3, k2tog, using MC, k1, ssk, k3, k2tog, k1. (*12 sts*)
Row 33: Purl, working colors as set.
Row 34: Using CC, ssk, k1, k2tog, using CC, k1, ssk, k1, k2tog, k1. (*8 sts*)
Divide rem sts evenly between two needles and, with RS tog and using third needle, bind (cast) off using three-needle bind (cast) off technique.

Ear
(make two)
Using MC, cast on 5 sts.
Starting with a k row, work 2 rows in st st.
Shaping is done with short rows.
Row 3: K4, turn.
Row 4: Slds, p2, turn.
Row 5: Slds, k to end.
Starting with a p row, work 3 rows in st st.
Bind (cast) off, leaving a length of yarn for sewing up.

Nose
Using A, cast on 5 sts.
Starting with a k row, work 2 rows in st st.
Row 3: Ssk, k1, k2tog. (*3 sts*)
Row 4: CDD.
Thread yarn through rem st to fasten off, leaving length of yarn for sewing up.

Making up
Add the safety eyes to the head by pushing through the knitting just below the eyebrows, using the photos as a guide for position. When you are happy with the placement, firmly push the backs onto the post of each eye.

Starting at the neck, sew the seam down the back of the body. Fold the base up and sew in place. Stuff with toy filling.

Stuff the head with toy filling and then pin it to the top of the body, matching the back seams. When you are happy with the placement, sew firmly in place.

Sew the side seam on the arm and stuff with toy filling. Repeat for second arm. Pin the arms in place with the seams facing downward, using the photos as a guide for position, then sew in place.

Sew the seam along the leg, fold the base of the foot up and sew in place. Stuff with toy filling. Pin the legs to the body, using the photos as a guide, then sew in place.

Fold ears in half and sew the seam closed and, as you sew, pull the ears into a rounded shape. Pin the ears to the top of the head and then sew in place.

Pin the nose to the front of the snout, placing a tiny amount of toy filling inside, and then sew in place. Embroider the mouth using straight stitches (see page 142) and A.

honey the sun bear 45

Skill Level ★ ★ ✶

mischief the chimpanzee

This cheeky little chap's face is knitted with a tiny amount of intarsia colorwork. Don't worry if you haven't used this technique before— it's only a few rows and is much easier than you think.

Yarn and materials
Rowan Felted Tweed (50% wool, 25% viscose, 25% alpaca) light worsted (DK) weight yarn, 191yd (175m) per 1¾oz (50g) ball
- ¾ ball of Phantom 153 (dark brown (MC)
- ⅛ ball of Camel shade 157 (light brown) (CC)

Small amount of black fingering (4-ply) weight yarn (or embroidery floss/thread) (A)

Pair of 8mm black with brown edge domed safety eyes

Toy filling

Needles and equipment
US 2 or 3 (3mm) knitting needles

Yarn needle

Scissors

Pins

Finished size
Base to top of head: 5½in (14cm)

Gauge (tension)
Approx 26 sts to 4in (10cm) measured over stockinette (stocking) stitch using US 2 or 3 (3mm) knitting needles.

Abbreviations
See page 143.

Pattern note
Wind a separate length of MC before you begin, for the intarsia section on the head.

Head
Start at bottom of lower face section.
Using CC, cast on 11 sts.
Row 1 (WS): Purl.
Row 2: K1, M1, k to last st, M1, k1. (*13 sts*)
Row 3: P1, M1, p to last st, M1, p1. (*15 sts*)
Shaping is done with short rows (see page 140).
Row 4: K13, turn.
Row 5: Slds, p10, turn.
Row 6: Slds, k9, turn.
Row 7: Slds, p8, turn.
Row 8: Slds, k7, turn.
Row 9: Slds, p6, turn.
Row 10: Slds, k to end.
Row 11: Purl.
Row 12: K1, M1, k3, M1, k7, M1, k3, M1, k1. (*19 sts*)
Row 13: Purl.
Row 14: K16, turn.
Row 15: Slds, p12, turn.
Row 16: Slds, k11, turn.
Row 17: Slds, p10, turn.
Row 18: Slds, k to end.
Row 19: Purl.
Row 20: K4, k2tog, k7, ssk, k4. (*17 sts*)
Row 21: P4, p2togtbl, p5, p2tog, p4. (*15 sts*)
Row 22: K4, k2tog, k3, ssk, k4. (*13 sts*)
Bind (cast) off.
Using CC, with RS facing, pick up and k 13 sts along bound- (cast-) off edge. Join in two separate lengths of MC and work in intarsia (see page 141).

Row 1: Using MC, p2, using CC, p9, using MC, p2.
Row 2: Using MC, k2, using CC, k9, using MC, k2.
Rep last 2 rows once more.
Cont using intarsia.
Row 5: Using MC, p2, using CC, p4, using MC, p1, using CC, p4, using MC, p2.
Row 6: Using MC, k3, using CC, k2, using MC, k3, using CC, k2, using MC, k3. Break off CC, cont in MC.
Starting with a p row, work 3 rows in st st.
Row 10: K1, ssk, k to last 3 sts, k2tog, k1. (*11 sts*)
Row 11: P1, p2tog, p5, turn. (*10 sts*)
Row 12: Slds, k4, turn.
Row 13: Slds, p to last 3 sts, p2togtbl, p1. (*9 sts*)
Row 14: K8, turn.
Row 15: Slds, p6, turn.
Row 16: Slds, k5, turn.
Row 17: Slds, p4, turn.
Row 18: Slds, k to end.
Row 19: Purl.
Row 20: K1, M1, k to last st, M1, k1. (*11 sts*)
Row 21: P1, M1, p to last st, M1, p1. (*13 sts*)
Row 22: K1, M1, k to last st, M1, k1. (*15 sts*)
Starting with a p row, work 15 rows in st st.
Row 38: K1, ssk, k to last 3 sts, k2tog, k1. (*13 sts*)
Row 39: P1, p2tog, p to last 3 sts, p2togtbl, p1. (*11 sts*)
Row 40: K1, ssk, k5, turn. (*10 sts*)
Row 41: Slds, p4, turn.
Row 42: Slds, k4, k2tog, k1. (*9 sts*)
Row 43: Purl.
Bind (cast) off.

mischief the chimpanzee 47

Body

Start at neck.
Using MC, cast on 20 sts.
Row 1 (WS): Purl.
Row 2: K9, M1, k2, M1, k9. (*22 sts*)
Row 3: Purl.
Row 4: K10, M1, k2, M1, k10. (*24 sts*)
Row 5: Purl.
Row 6: K10, M1, k4, M1, k10. (*26 sts*)
Row 7: Purl.
Row 8: K2, M1, k8, M1, k6, M1, k8, M1, k2. (*30 sts*)
Row 9: Purl.
Row 10: K2, M1, k9, M1, k8, M1, k9, M1, k2. (*34 sts*)
Row 11: Purl.
Shaping is done with short rows.
Row 12: K2, M1, k10, M1, k10, turn. (*36 sts*)
Row 13: Slds, p9, turn.
Row 14: Slds, k8, turn.
Row 15: Slds, p7, turn.
Row 16: Slds, k8, M1, k10, M1, k2. (*38 sts*)
Row 17: Purl.
Row 18: K2, M1, k11, M1, k12, M1, k11, M1, k2. (*42 sts*)
Row 19: Purl.
Row 20: K2, M1, k12, M1, k14, M1, k12, M1, k2. (*46 sts*)
Starting with a p row, work 5 rows in st st.
Row 26: K2, ssk, k23, turn.
Row 27: Slds, p7, turn.
Row 28: Slds, k to last 4 sts, k2tog, k2. (*44 sts*)
Row 29: P2, p2tog, p to last 4 sts, p2togtbl, p2. (*42 sts*)
Row 30: Knit.
Rep Rows 29 and 30 once more. (*40 sts*)
Row 33: Purl.
Cont working in st st and bind (cast) off 15 sts at beg of next 2 rows. (*10 sts*)
Cont making base.
Row 36: K2, M1, k to last 2 sts, M1, k2. (*12 sts*)
Starting with a p row, work 9 rows in st st.
Row 46: K1, ssk, k6, k2tog, k1. (*10 sts*)
Row 47: Purl.
Row 48: K1, ssk, k4, k2tog, k1. (*8 sts*)
Row 49: P1, p2tog, p2, p2togtbl, k1. (*6 sts*)
Row 50: Knit.
Bind (cast) off.

Left arm and leg

(make 2)
Using MC, cast on 4 sts.
Row 1 (WS): Purl.
Row 2: K1, M1, k to last st, M1, k1. (*6 sts*)
Row 3: Purl.
Rep Rows 2 and 3 three more times. (*12 sts*)
Shaping is done with short rows.
*Row 10: K9, turn.
Row 11: Slds, p5, turn.
Row 12: Slds, k to end.
Row 13: Purl.**

Starting with a k row, work 2 rows in st st.*
Rep from * to * once more.
Work from * to ** once.
Row 26: K2, ssk, k4, k2tog, k2. (*10 sts*)
Row 27: Purl.
Change to CC.
Row 28: Knit.
Row 29: P3, M1, p4, M1, p3. (*12 sts*)
Starting with a k row, work 2 rows in st st.
Beg working thumb at edge of row only.
Row 32: K1, M1, k1, wyib sl 3 sts from RH needle to LH needle.
Row 33: Do not turn, pull yarn across back of work, k3, wyib sl 3 sts from RH needle to LH needle.
Row 34: Do not turn, pull yarn across back of work, k3, thread yarn through sts and fasten off, leaving length of yarn for sewing up.
With RS facing, rejoin CC to next st on needle, k to end. (*10 sts*)
Starting with a p row, work 2 rows in st st.
Next row: [P2tog] 5 times. (*5 sts*)
Thread yarn through rem sts to fasten off, leaving length of yarn for sewing up.

Right arm and leg

(make 2)
Using MC, cast on 4 sts.
Row 1 (WS): Purl.
Row 2: K1, M1, k to last st, M1, k1. (*6 sts*)
Row 3: Purl.
Rep Rows 2 and 3 three more times. (*12 sts*)
Shaping is done with short rows.

forests and jungles

*Row 10: K9, turn.
Row 11: Slds, p5, turn.
Row 12: Slds, k to end.
Row 13: Purl.**
Starting with a k row, work 2 rows in st st.*
Rep from * to * once more.
Work from * to ** once.
Row 26: K2, ssk, k4, k2tog, k2. (*10 sts*)
Row 27: Purl.
Change to CC.
Row 28: Knit.
Row 29: P3, M1, p4, M1, p3. (*12 sts*)
Starting with a k row, work 2 rows in st st.
Beg working thumb at edge of row only.
Row 32: K11, M1, k1, wyib sl 3 sts from RH needle to LH
needle.
Row 33: Do not turn, pull yarn across back of work, k3, wyib
sl 3 sts from RH needle to LH needle.
Row 34: Do not turn, pull yarn across back of work, k3,
thread yarn through sts and fasten off, leaving length of yarn
for sewing up.
With RS facing, rejoin CC to next st on needle, p to end.
(*10 sts*)
Starting with a k row, work 2 rows in st st.
Next row: [K2tog] 5 times. (*5 sts*)
Thread yarn through rem sts to fasten off, leaving length of
yarn for sewing up.

Ear

(make 2)
Using CC, cast on 4 sts.
Starting with a k row, work 4 rows in st st.
Shaping is done with short rows.
Row 5: K3, turn.
Row 6: Slds, p1, turn.
Row 7: Slds, k to end.
Starting with a p row, work 3 rows in st st.
Bind (cast) off, leaving length of yarn for sewing up.

Nose

Using MC, cast on 3 sts.
Row 1: [K1, M1] twice, k1. (*5 sts*)
Row 2: Purl.
Row 3: Ssk, k1, k2tog. (*3 sts*)
Bind (cast) off, leaving length of yarn for sewing up.

Tail

Using MC, cast on 4 sts.
Row 1: Purl.
Row 2: K1, M1, k to last st, M1, k1. (*6 sts*)
Row 3: Purl.
Rep Rows 2 and 3 once more. (*8 sts*)
Starting with a k row, work 8 rows in st st.
Shaping is done with short rows.
*Row 14: K7, turn.
Row 15: Slds, p5, turn.

Row 16: Slds, k to end.
Row 17: Purl.*
Starting with a k row, work 2 rows in st st.**
Work from * to ** 3 more times.
Work from * to * 5 times.
Row 58: K1, ssk, k2, k2tog, k1. (*6 sts*)
Row 59: Purl.
Row 60: [K2tog] 3 times. (*5 sts*)
Thread yarn through rem sts to fasten off, leaving length of yarn
for sewing up.

Making up

Pin the head together and stuff with toy filling. Push each of
the eyes through the knitting and check they are in the correct
place, using the photos as a guide. Once you are happy with
their placement, remove the pins and toy filling and push the
backs of the eyes firmly onto the post of each eye. Re-stuff
with toy filling and sew the bottom seam of the head together.
Fold the ear in half with WS together and sew the cast-on and
bound- (cast-) off edges together.

Repeat for the second ear. Using the photos for guidance,
pin the ears in place on each side of the head and, when you
are happy with their placement, sew in place. Pin the nose to
the head with the cast-on and bound- (cast-) off edges close
together to make the nose stand out. Sew in place.

Sew the seam along the back of the body. Fold the base up
and sew to the bottom edge of the body, stuffing with toy filling
as you go. Sew the head to the body.

Using MC yarn, sew the side seam on an arm/leg that will be
facing the body when you sew the arms and legs on. Stuff with
toy filling as you go. Change to CC yarn and sew the hand and
thumb together, stuffing the hand with toy filling. Repeat for the
three other limbs. Pin the arms and legs to the body using the
photos for guidance. Sew firmly to the body.

Sew the side seam of the tail, stuffing with toy filling as
you go to make the tail curl. Using the photos as a guide for
position, sew the tail to the body. Using A, embroider the mouth
using straight stitches (see page 142).

TIP The short row shaping gives a lovely curly tail.
If you aren't giving the chimp to a small child, you
could thread a chenille stick (pipe cleaner) along
the tail so you can bend it into the curly shape.

mischief the chimpanzee 49

Skill Level ★ ★ ★

bandit the ring-tailed lemur

You will need a small piece of orange felt to place behind the
eyes to give your ring-tailed lemur their inquisitive look.

Yarn and materials
Rowan Felted Tweed (50% wool, 25%
viscose, 25% alpaca) light worsted (DK)
weight yarn, 191yd (175m) per 1¾oz
(50g) ball
   1 ball of Carbon 159 (dark gray) (MC)
   ¼ ball of Black 211 (CC1)
   ¼ ball of Alabaster 197 (gray) (CC2)
Small amount of black fingering
(4-ply) yarn
Pair of 5mm black domed safety eyes
Small piece of orange felt
Toy filling

Needles and equipment
US 2 or 3 (3mm) knitting needles
Spare knitting needle for three-needle
bind (cast) off
Yarn needle
Scissors
Pins

Finished size
Base to top of head seated: 6¼in (16cm)

Gauge (tension)
Approx 26 sts to 4in (10cm) measured
over stockinette (stocking) stitch using
US 2 or 3 (3mm) knitting needles.

Abbreviations
See page 143.

Pattern note
Wind separate small balls of MC and
CC2 before you begin, for the intarsia
sections on the head and body.

Head
Start at nose.
Using CC1, cast on 10 sts.
Row 1 (RS): K4, M1, k2, M1, k4. (*12 sts*)
Row 2: P4, M1, p4, M1, p4. (*14 sts*)
Row 3: K4, M1, k6, M1, k4. (*16 sts*)
Row 4: P4, M1, p8, M1, p4. (*18 sts*)
Row 5: K4, M1, k10, M1, k4. (*20 sts*)
Row 6: Purl.
Change to CC2 yarn.
Row 7: Knit.
Row 8: [P2, M1] four times, p4, [M1, p2] four times. (*28 sts*)
Row 9: Knit.
Join in two separate strands of MC and two of CC2 and work
in intarsia (see page 141).
Row 10: Using CC2, p10, using MC, p3, using CC2, p2, using
MC, p3, using CC2, p10.
Row 11: Using CC2, k9, using MC, k4, using CC2, k2, using
MC, k4, using CC2, k9.
Row 12: Using CC2, [p2, M1] four times, using MC, p5, using
CC2, p2, using MC, p5, using CC2, [M1, p2] 4 times. (*36 sts*)
Row 13: Using CC2, k12, using MC, k5, using CC2, k2, using
MC, k5, using CC2, k12.
Row 14: Using CC2, [p3, M1] four times, using MC, p4, using
CC2, p4, using MC, p4, using CC2, [M1, p3] 4 times. (*44 sts*)
Row 15: Using CC2, k16, using MC, k3, using CC2, k6, using
MC, k3, using CC2, k16.
Break off one strand of MC, cont using CC2.
Starting with a p row, work 2 rows in st st.

Row 18: Using CC2, p13, M1, p1, M1, p5, using MC, p6, using
CC2, p5, M1, p1, M1, p13. (48 sts)
Row 19: Using CC2, k19, using MC, k10, using CC2, k19.
Row 20: Using CC2, p16, using MC, p16, using CC2, p16.
Break off CC2, cont in MC.
Starting with a k row, work 2 rows in st st.
Row 23: [K3, ssk] four times, k8, [k2tog, k3] four times. (*40 sts*)
Row 24: Purl.
Row 25: [K3, ssk] three times, k10, [k2tog, k3] three times.
(*34 sts*)
Row 26: Purl.
Row 27: [K2, ssk] four times, k2, [k2tog, k2] four times. (*26 sts*)
Row 28: Purl.
Row 29: [K2, ssk] three times, k2, [k2tog, k2] three times.
(*20 sts*)
Row 30: Purl.
Divide rem sts evenly between two needles and, with RS tog and
using third needle, bind (cast) off using three-needle bind (cast)
off technique (see page 139).

Body
Start at neck.
Using CC2 yarn, cast on 26 sts.
Join in two separate lengths of MC and work in intarsia.
Row 1: Using MC, k7, using CC2, k12, using MC, k7.
Row 2: Using MC, p7, using CC2, p12, using MC, p7.
Rep last 2 rows twice more.
Row 7: Using MC, k6, M1, k1, using CC2, k1, M1, k10, M1, k1,
using MC, k1, M1, k6. (30 sts)
Row 8: Using MC, p8, using CC2, p14, using MC, p8.

50   **forests and jungles**

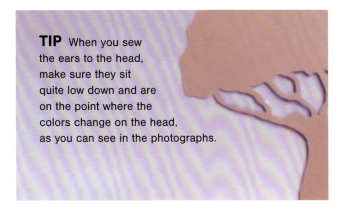

TIP When you sew the ears to the head, make sure they sit quite low down and are on the point where the colors change on the head, as you can see in the photographs.

Row 9: Using MC, k8, using CC2, k14, using MC, k8.
Row 10: Using MC, p8, using CC2, p14, using MC, p8.
Row 11: Using MC, k7, M1, k1, using CC2, k1, M1, k12, M1, k1, using MC, k1, M1, k7. (*34 sts*)
Row 12: Using MC, p9, using CC2, p16, using MC, p9.
Row 13: Using MC, k9, using CC2, k16, using MC, k9.
Row 14: Using MC, p9, using CC2, p16, using MC, p9.
Row 15: Using MC, k8, M1, k1, using CC2, k1, M1, k14, M1, k1, using MC, k1, M1, k8. (*38 sts*)
Starting with a p row, work 5 rows in st st.
Row 21: Using MC, k9, M1, k1, using CC2, k1, M1, k6, M1, k4, M1, k6, M1, k1, using MC, k1, M1, k9. (*44 sts*)
Row 22: Using MC, p11, using CC2, p22, using MC, p11.
Row 23: Using MC, k11, using CC2, k8, M1, k6, M1, k8, using MC, k11. (*46 sts*)
Starting with a p row, work 5 rows in st st.
Row 29: Using MC, k11, using CC2, k1, ssk, k18, k2tog, k1, using MC, k11. (*44 sts*)
Row 30: Using MC, p11, using CC2, p22, using MC, p11.
Row 31: Using MC, k8, ssk, k1, using CC2, k1, ssk, k3, ssk, k6, ssk, k3, ssk, k1, using MC, k1, k2tog, k8. (*38 sts*)
Starting with a p row, work 3 rows in st st.
Row 35: Using MC, k7, ssk, k1, using CC2, k1, ssk, k2, ssk, k4, k2tog, k2, k2tog, k1, using MC, k1, ssk, k7. (*32 sts*)
Row 36: Using MC, p9, using CC2, p14, using MC, p9.
Row 37: Using MC, bind (cast) off 9 sts, using CC2, bind (cast) off 3 sts, then k10, using MC, k9. (*20 sts*)
Row 38: Using MC, bind (cast) off 9 sts, using CC2, bind (cast) off 3 sts, then p7. (*8 sts*)
Break off MC, cont using CC2.
Row 39: K1, M1, k6, M1, k1. (*10 sts*)
Row 40: Purl.
Rep last 2 rows twice more. (*14 sts*)
Starting with a k row, work 4 rows in st st.
Row 48: K1, ssk, k to last 3 sts, k2tog, k1. (*12 sts*)
Row 49: Purl.
Rep last 2 rows twice more. (*8 sts*)
Bind (cast) off.

Leg and foot

(make 2)
Using CC2 yarn, cast on 16 sts.
Starting with a k row, work 12 rows in st st.
Change to CC1.
Row 13: K5, M1, [k2, M1] three times, k5. (*20 sts*)
Starting with a p row, work 5 rows in st st.
Row 19: [K2, ssk] twice, k1, k2tog, k1, [k2tog, k2] twice. (*15 sts*)
Row 20: Purl.
Row 21: K2, ssk, k1, ssk, k1, k2tog, k1, k2tog, k2. (*11 sts*)
Row 22: Purl.
Bind (cast) off.

Right arm

*Using MC, cast on 4 sts.
Row 1 (WS): Purl.
Row 2: K1, M1, k to last st, M1, k1. (*6 sts*)
Row 3: Purl.
Rep last 2 rows once more. (*8 sts*)
Starting with a k row, work 24 rows in st st.
Row 30: K1, ssk, k2, k2tog, k1. (*6 sts*)
Row 31: Purl.
Rep last 2 rows once more. (*4 sts*)
Beg paw for inner arm
Break off MC, join CC1.
Starting with a k row, work 2 rows in st st.
Row 36: K1, M1, k2, M1, k1. (*6 sts*)
Starting with a p row, work 3 rows in st st. Break off CC1, join CC2.
Starting with a k row, work 8 rows in st st.*
Shaping is done with short rows (see page 140).
Row 48: K4, turn.
Row 49: Slds, p to end.
Row 50: K3, turn.
Row 51: Slds, p to end.
Starting with a k row, work 4 rows in st st. Bind (cast) off.

Left arm

Work as for right arm from * to *.
Row 48: Knit.
Shaping is done with short rows.
Row 49: P4, turn.
Row 50: Slds, k to end.
Row 51: P3, turn.
Row 52: Slds, k to end.
Starting with a k row, work 4 rows in st st. Bind (cast) off.

Tail

Using CC2, cast on 6 sts.
Row 1 (WS): Purl.
Row 2: K1, M1, k4, M1, k1. (*8 sts*)
Row 3: Purl.
Row 4: Cast on 3 sts, k to end. (*11 sts*)
Row 5: Cast on 3 sts, p to end. (*14 sts*)
Starting with a k row, work 2 rows in st st.

Change to CC1, starting with a k row, work 4 rows in st st.
Change to CC2, starting with a k row, work 4 rows in st st.
Rep last 8 rows four more times.
Change to CC1, starting with a k row, work 4 rows in st st.
Change to CC2, cont as foll:
Row 52: [K1, k2tog] four times, k2. (*10 sts*)
Row 53: Purl.
Row 54: [K2tog] five times. (*5 sts*)
Row 55: Purl.
Thread yarn through rem sts to fasten off, leaving length of yarn for sewing up.

Inner ear
(make 2)
Using MC, cast on 3 sts.
Row 1 (RS): [K1, M1] twice, k1. (*5 sts*)
Row 2: Purl.
Rep last 2 rows three more times. (*11 sts*)
Bind (cast) off.

Outer ear
(make 2)
Using CC2, cast on 6 sts.
Starting with a k row, work 2 rows in st st.
Row 3: Ssk, k2, k2tog. (*4 sts*)
Row 4: Purl.
Row 5: Ssk, k2tog. (*2 sts*)
Row 6: P2tog. (*1 st*)
Thread yarn through rem st, leaving length of yarn for sewing up.

Nose
Using A, cast on 5 sts.
Starting with a k row, work 2 rows in st st.
Row 3: Ssk, k1, k2tog. (*3 sts*)
Row 4: CDD. (*1 st*)
Thread yarn through rem st to fasten off, leaving length of yarn for sewing up.

Making up
Cut two ⅜in (1cm) squares of orange felt. Fold one in half and make a small cut in the center with sharp scissors, just large enough for the back of the safety eye to thread through. Thread the post of the eye through the hole and then trim the felt to leave a 1/16in (2mm) border around the outside of the eye. Repeat for the second eye. Push the safety eyes through the knitting using the photos as a guide for position. When you are happy with their placement, firmly push the back onto the post of each eye.

Using matching yarn and starting at the nose, sew the seam underneath the head. Stuff with toy filling and sew the seam closed at the back of the head. Using a needle threaded with MC, push it from the base of the head, underneath one eye and back down to the base, pulling the yarn to tighten. Repeat for second eye and then secure the yarn. This will give a more realistic look to the face.

Starting at the neck, sew the seam that runs down the back of the body. Fold the base up and sew in place. Stuff with toy filling. Pin the head to the top of the body, matching the back seams and different colored sections. When you are happy with the placement, sew firmly in place.

Fold an arm in half at the start of the paw and sew the side seam closed, stuffing with toy filling as you go. Repeat for the second arm. Pin the arms in place on each side of the body, using the photos for guidance, then sew in place.

Using matching yarn, sew the seam along the leg, changing color to sew the foot together. Stuff with toy filling. Repeat for the second leg. Pin the legs to the body, using the photos as a guide for position, and then sew in place.

With WS together, sew an inner ear to the lower edge and one side to an outer ear. On the free side, fold the top of the outer ear over and sew in place along the lower edge of the ear. Repeat to make a match for the second ear. Pin the ears in place on each side of the head and, when you are happy with their placement, sew in place.

Pin the nose to the front of the face, place a tiny amount of toy filling inside and then sew in place.

Gather and sew the bound- (cast-) off edge of the tail closed and sew the seam. Pin cast-on edge in place on the back of the body, ensuring the tail sits sideways, as in the photos. Sew in place.

bandit the ring-tailed lemur 53

Skill Level ★ ★ ★

dumpling the panda

This cuddly panda has eye patches knitted using the intarsia technique, which stops the stitches "bunching up" in between the eye patches, giving a really neat result. Just add toy filling to the feet and not the legs to make your panda even more cuddly.

Yarn and materials

Sirdar Haworth Tweed (50% merino wool, 50% nylon) light worsted (DK) weight yarn, 180yd (165m) per 1¾oz (50g) ball

  ¾ ball of Hepworth Slate 901 (black) (MC)

  ¼ ball of Cotton Grass Cream 911 (cream) (CC)

Small amount of black fingering (4-ply) weight yarn (A)

Pair of 5mm black domed safety eyes

Toy filling

Needles and equipment

US 2 or 3 (3mm) knitting needles

Yarn needle

Scissors

Pins

Finished size

Toe to top of head: 8¾in (22cm) standing

Base to top of head: 6in (15cm) seated

Gauge (tension)

Approx 26 sts to 4in (10cm) measured over stockinette (stocking) stitch using US 2 or 3 (3mm) knitting needles.

Abbreviations

See page 143.

Pattern note

Wind separate small balls of MC and CC before you begin, for the intarsia sections on the head and body.

Head

Start at neck.

Using CC, cast on 36 sts.

Row 1 (WS): Purl.

Row 2: K8, M1, k1, M1, k7, M1, k4, M1, k7, M1, k1, M1, k8. (*42 sts*)

Row 3: Purl.

Row 4: K9, M1, k1, M1, k9, M1, k4, M1, k9, M1, k1, M1, k9. (*48 sts*)

Row 5: Purl.

Row 6: K22, M1, k4, M1, k22. (*50 sts*)

Row 7: Purl.

FACE MARKINGS

Join in two separate strands of MC, beg intarsia technique (see page 141) to carry CC across back of each eye marking.

Row 8: Using CC, k20, using MC, k2, using CC, k6, using MC, k2, using CC, k20.

Row 9: Using CC, p20, using MC, p3, using CC, p4, using MC, p3, using CC, p20.

Row 10: Using CC, k20, using MC, k3, using CC, k4, using MC, k3, using CC, k20.

Row 11: Using CC, p20, using MC, p4, using CC, p2, using MC, p4, using CC, p20.

Row 12: Using CC, k21, using MC, k3, using CC, k2, using MC, k3, using CC, k21.

Row 13: Using CC, p22, using MC, p2, using CC, p2, using MC, p2, using CC, p22.

Break off MC, cont in CC only.

Starting with a k row, work 4 rows in st st.

Row 18: K9, ssk, k1, k2tog, k22, ssk, k1, k2tog, k9. (*46 sts*)

Row 19: Purl.

Row 20: K8, ssk, k1, k2tog, k20, ssk, k1, k2tog, k8. (*42 sts*)

Row 21: Purl.

Row 22: K7, ssk, k1, k2tog, k18, ssk, k1, k2tog, k7. (*38 sts*)

Row 23: P9, p2togtbl, p16, p2tog, p9. (*36 sts*)

Row 24: K6, ssk, k1, k2tog, k14, ssk, k1, k2tog, k6. (*32 sts*)

Row 25: P8, p2togtbl, p12, p2tog, p8. (*30 sts*)

Bind (cast) off.

dumpling the panda 55

Body

Start at base.

Using CC, cast on 10 sts.

Row 1: Purl.

Row 2: K2, M1, k to last 2 sts, M1, k2. (*12 sts*)

Row 3: Purl.

Rep Rows 2 and 3 three more times. (*18 sts*)

Starting with a k row, work 8 rows in st st.

Row 18: K2, ssk, k to last 4 sts, k2tog, k2. (*16 sts*)

Row 19: Purl.

Rep Rows 18 and 19 once more. (*14 sts*)

Row 22: K2, ssk, k to last 4 sts, k2tog, k2. (*12 sts*)

Row 23: P2, p2tog, p to last 4 sts, p2togtbl, p2. (*10 sts*)

Row 24: K2, ssk, k2, k2tog, k2. (*8 sts*)

Row 25: Purl.

Cont in st st and cast on 19 sts at beg of next 2 rows. (*46 sts*)

Starting with a k row, work 2 rows in st st.

Row 30: K12, M1, k8, M1, k6, M1, k8, M1, k12. (*50 sts*)

Row 31: Purl.

Row 32: K12, M1, k1, M1, k9, M1, k6, M1, k9, M1, k1, M1, k12. (*56 sts*)

Row 33: Purl.

Row 34: K25, M1, k6, M1, k25. (*58 sts*)

Starting with a p row, work 9 rows in st st.

Row 44: K12, ssk, k1, k2tog, k24, ssk, k1, k2tog, k12. (*54 sts*)

Row 45: Purl.

BODY MARKINGS

Join in two separate strands of CC, beg intarsia technique to carry CC across back of each marking.

Row 46: Using CC, k10, using MC, k7, using CC, k20, using MC, k7, using CC, k10.

Row 47: Using CC, p9, using MC, p9, using CC, p18, using MC, p9, using CC, p9.

Row 48: Using CC, k8, using MC, k3, ssk, k1, k2tog, k3, using CC, k3, ssk, k6, k2tog, k3, using MC, k3, ssk, k1, k2tog, k3, using CC, k8. (*48 sts*)

Row 49: Using CC, p7, using MC, p11, using CC, p12, using MC, p11, using CC, p7.

Row 50: Using CC, k6, using MC, k13, using CC, k10, using MC, k13, using CC, k6.

Row 51: Using CC, p5, using MC, p15, using CC, p8, using MC, p15, using CC, p5.

Row 52: Using CC, k4, using MC, k6, ssk, k1, k2tog, k6, using CC, ssk, k2, k2tog, using MC, k6, ssk, k1, k2tog, k6, using CC, k4. (*42 sts*)

Break off CC, cont in MC only.

Starting with a p row, work 3 rows in st st.

Bind (cast) off.

Left arm

Using MC, cast on 4 sts.

Row 1 (WS): Purl.

Row 2: K1, M1, k to last st, M1, k1. (*6 sts*)

Row 3: Purl.

Rep Rows 2 and 3 once more. (*8 sts*)

Cont in st st and cast on 8 sts at beg of next row. (*16 sts*)

Starting with a p row, work 7 rows in st st.

Shaping is done with short rows (see page 140).

Row 14: K4, turn.

Row 15: Slds, p to end.

Row 16: Knit.

Row 17: P4, turn.

Row 18: Slds, k to end.

Row 19: Purl.

Starting with a k row, work 8 rows in st st.

Row 28: K1, ssk, k2, k2tog, k2, ssk, k2, k2tog, k1. (*12 sts*)

Row 29: Purl.

Row 30: K1, ssk, k2, k2tog, k2, ssk, k2, k2tog, k1. (*12 sts*)

Thread yarn through rem st to fasten off, leaving length of yarn for sewing up.

Right arm

Using MC, cast on 4 sts.

Row 1 (RS): Knit.

Row 2: P1, M1, p to last st, M1, p1. (*6 sts*)

Row 3: Knit.

Rep Rows 2 and 3 once more. (*8 sts*)

Cast on 8 sts at beg of next row. (*16 sts*)

Starting with a k row, work 7 rows in st st.

Shaping is done with short rows.

Row 14: P4, turn.

Row 15: Slds, k to end.

Row 16: Purl.

Row 17: K4, turn.

Row 18: Slds, p to end.

Row 19: Knit.

Starting with a p row, work 7 rows in st st.

Row 27: K1, ssk, k2, k2tog, k2, ssk, k2, k2tog, k1. (*12 sts*)

Row 28: Purl.

Row 29: K1, ssk, k2tog, k2, ssk, k2tog, k1. (*8 sts*)

Thread yarn through rem st to fasten off, leaving length of yarn for sewing up.

TIP There is just a small amount of short row shaping in this pattern, so if you haven't tried it before, this would be a good project to start with.

Leg and foot

(make 2)
Using MC, cast on 18 sts.
Starting with a k row, work 10 rows in st st.
Row 11: K8, M1, k2, M1, k8. (*20 sts*)
Row 12: P9, M1, p2, M1, p9. (*22 sts*)
Row 13: K10, M1, k2, M1, k10. (*24 sts*)
Row 14: P11, M1, p2, M1, p11. (*62 sts*)
Cont in st st and bind (cast) off 11 sts at beg of next 2 rows. (*4 sts*)
Row 17: K1, M1, k to last st, M1, k1. (*6 sts*)
Row 18: Purl.
Rep Rows 17 and 18 once more. (*8 sts*)
Starting with a k row, work 4 rows in st st.
Row 25: K1, ssk, k to last 3 sts, k2tog, k1. (*6 sts*)
Row 26: Purl.
Rep Rows 25 and 26 once more. (*4 sts*)
Bind (cast) off.

Ear

(make 2)
Using MC, cast on 5 sts.
Starting with a k row, work 2 rows in st st.
Shaping is done with short rows.
Row 3: K4, turn.
Row 4: Slds, p2, turn.
Row 5: Slds, k to end.
Row 6: Purl.
Bind (cast) off, leaving length of yarn for sewing up.

Nose

Using A, cast on 5 sts.
Starting with a k row, work 2 rows in st st.
Row 3: Ssk, k1, k2tog. (*3 sts*)
Row 4: CDD.
Thread yarn through rem st to fasten off, leaving length of yarn for sewing up.

Making up

Add the safety eyes to the head by pushing through the knitting on upper face marking, using the photos as a guide for position. When you are happy with the placement, firmly push the backs onto the post of each eye. Sew the back seam of the head and, folding the seam at the top of the head so that the seam is in the middle of the back, sew the top seam of the head together and stuff with toy filling.

Starting at the neck, sew the seam along the back of the body. Stuff with toy filling and pin the base to the lower edge of the body. Sew the base in place, adding more toy filling if necessary.

Pin the head to the top of the body, overlapping the top of the body and matching the back seams.

Sew the small side seam that will be at the back of each leg and then sew the base of the foot in place. Stuff the foot with toy filling, leaving the leg unstuffed. Sew the cast-on edge together horizontally and pin in place, using the photos for guidance. Sew each leg and foot in place.

Fold ears in half. Sew the seam on the ears closed and, as you sew, pull the ears into a rounded shape. Pin the ears to the top of the head and, when you are happy with their placement, sew in place.

Pin the nose to the front of the head and sew in place. Using A, embroider the mouth using straight stitches (see page 142).

dumpling the panda

Skill Level ★ ★ ★

saber the tiger

Would you ask this tiger to tea? His thin black stripes are knitted as you work each part of the body, with the final markings on the face embroidered on afterward.

Yarn and materials
Rowan Felted Tweed (50% wool, 25% viscose, 25% alpaca) light worsted (DK) weight yarn, 191yd (175m) per 1¾oz (50g) ball
- 1 ball of Ginger 154 (orange) (MC)
- ½ ball of Treacle 145 (dark brown) (CC1)
- ½ ball of Clay 177 (off-white) (CC2)

Small amount of black fingering (4-ply) weight yarn (A)

Needles and equipment
US 2 or 3 (3mm) knitting needles

Spare knitting needles

Yarn needle

Scissors

Pins

Finished size
Top of head to toe: 9½in (24cm)

Gauge (tension)
Approx 26 sts to 4in (10cm) measured over stockinette (stocking) stitch using US 2 or 3 (3mm) knitting needles.

Abbreviations
See page 143.

Pattern notes
Some of the shaping in this pattern is done using German short rows with the abbreviation slds (see page 140). The ears are shaped by slipping a stitch, which is worked together with the following stitch on the next row.

Wind separate small balls of MC, CC1, and CC2 before you begin, for the intarsia sections on the head and body.

Head
Start at nose.
Using CC1 yarn, cast on 3 sts.
Row 1 (WS): Purl.
Row 2: [K1, M1] twice, k1. (*5 sts*)
Row 3: Purl.
Rep last 2 rows once more. (*7 sts*)
Row 6: Knit.
Row 7: Purl.
Break yarn and leave sts on a spare needle.

Muzzle
SIDE 1
Using CC2 yarn, cast on 7 sts.
Row 1 (WS): Purl.
Row 2: K to last st, M1, k1. (*8 sts*)
Row 3: Purl.
Rep last 2 rows once more. (*9 sts*)
Break yarn and leave sts on a spare needle.
SIDE 2
Using CC2 yarn, cast on 7 sts.
Row 1 (WS): Purl.
Row 2: K1, M1, k to end. (*8 sts*)
Row 3: Purl.
Rep last 2 rows once more. (*9 sts*)
Join in another ball of CC2.
Row 6: Using CC2, k9, with RS facing and using CC1, k across 7 held nose sts, with RS facing and using CC2, k across side 1 of muzzle. (*25 sts*)
Row 7: Using CC2, p9, using MC, p7, using CC2, p9.

Row 8: Using CC2, k7, using MC, k11, using CC2, k7.
Row 9: Using CC2, p6, using MC, p13, using CC2, p6.
Row 10: Using CC2, k3, M1, k2, using MC, k3, M1, k9, M1, k3, using CC2, k2, M1, k3. (*29 sts*)
Row 11: Using CC2, p5, using MC, p19, using CC2, p5.
Shaping is done with short rows.
Row 12: Using CC2, k4, using MC, k5, turn.
Row 13: Using MC, slds, p5, turn.
Row 14: Using MC, slds, k22, turn.
Row 15: Using MC slds, p5, turn.
Row 16: Using MC, slds, k5, using CC2, k4.
Row 17: Using CC2, p3, using MC, p23, using CC2, p3.
Break off CC2 yarn and work as foll, joining in CC1 as directed:
Row 18: Using CC1, k4, M1, k5, using MC, M1, k11, M1, using CC1, k5, M1, k4. (*33 sts*)
Break off CC1, cont using MC.
Row 19: Purl.
Row 20: K4, M1, k7, M1, k11, M1, k7, M1, k4. (*37 sts*)
Row 21: Purl.
Row 22: Using CC1, k13, using MC, k3, M1, k5, M1, k3, using CC1, k13. (*39 sts*)
Break off CC1, cont using MC.
Row 23: Purl.
Row 24: K17, M1, k5, M1, k17. (*41 sts*)
Row 25: Purl.
Row 26: K24, turn.
Row 27: Slds, p6, turn.
Row 28: Slds, k to end.
Row 29: Purl.
Row 30: Using CC1, k16, using MC, k9, using CC1, k16.

58   forests and jungles

Break off CC1, cont using MC.
Row 31: K2, ssk, k12, ssk, k5, k2tog, k12, k2tog, k2. (*37 sts*)
Row 32: Purl.
Row 33: K2, ssk, k10, ssk, k5, k2tog, k10, k2tog, k2. (*33 sts*)
Row 34: Purl.
Row 35: K2, ssk, k8, ssk, k5, k2tog, k8, k2tog, k2. (*29 sts*)
Row 36: Purl.
Row 37: K2, ssk, k6, ssk, k5, k2tog, k6, k2tog, k2. (*25 sts*)
Row 38: Purl.
Bind (cast) off.

Body
Using MC, cast on 10 sts.
Row 1 (WS): Purl.
Row 2: K1, M1, k to last st, M1, k1. (*12 sts*)
Row 3: Purl.
Rep Rows 2 and 3 twice more. (*16 sts*)
Row 8: Knit.
Row 9: Purl.
Rep Rows 8 and 9 four more times.
Row 18: K1, ssk, k to last 3 sts, k2tog, k1. (*14 sts*)
Row 19: Purl.
Rep Rows 18 and 19 once more. (*12 sts*)
Row 22: Cast on 16 sts, k to end. (*28 sts*)
Row 23: Cast on 16 sts, p to end. (*44 sts*)
Row 24: Knit.
Row 25: Purl.
Row 26: K19, M1, k6, M1, k19. (*46 sts*)
Row 27: Purl.

Join in CC2 and another ball of MC and work in intarsia (see page 141).
Row 28: Using MC, k20, using CC2, k6, using CC1, k20.
Row 29: Using MC, p19, using CC2, p8, using MC, p19.
Join in two balls of CC1.
Row 30: Using CC1, k18, using CC2, k10, using MC, k18.
Row 31: Using MC, p17, using CC2, p12, using MC, p17.
Row 32: Using MC, k16, using CC2, k14, using MC, k16.
Row 33: Using MC, p16, using CC2, p14, using MC, p16.
Row 34: Using MC, k16, using CC2, k14, using MC, k16.
Row 35: Using CC1, p18, using CC2, p10, using CC1, p18.
Row 36: Using MC, k16, using CC2, k14, using MC, k16.
Row 37: Using MC, p16, using CC2, p14, using MC, p16.
Row 38: Using MC, k16, using CC2, k14, using MC, k16.
Row 39: Using MC, p16, using CC2, p14, using MC, p16.
Row 40: Using CC1, k18, using CC2, k10, using CC1, k18.
Row 41: Using MC, p16, using CC2, p14, using MC, p16.
Row 42: Using MC, k9, ssk, k1, k2tog, k2, using CC2, k1, ssk, k8, k2tog, k1, using MC, k2, ssk, k1, k2tog, k9. (*40 sts*)
Row 43: Using MC, p14, using CC2, p12, using MC, p14.
Row 44: Using MC, k14, using CC2, k12, using MC, k14.
Row 45: Using CC1, p16, using CC2, p8, using CC1, p16.
Row 46: Using MC, k8, ssk, k1, k2tog, k1, using CC2, k1, ssk, k6, k2tog, k1, using MC, k1, ssk, k1, k2tog, k8. (*34 sts*)
Row 47: Using MC, p12, using CC2, p10, using MC, p12.
Row 48: Using MC, k7, ssk, k1, k2tog, using CC2, k1, ssk, k4, k2tog, k1, using MC, ssk, k1, k2tog, k7. (*28 sts*)
Row 49: Using MC, p10, using CC2, p8, using MC, p10.
Row 50: Using CC1, k12, using CC2, k4, using CC1, k12.
Row 51: Using MC, p10, using CC2, p8, using MC, p10.
Row 52: Using MC, k8, ssk, using CC2, k1, ssk, k2, k2tog, k1, using CC1, ssk, k8. (*24 sts*)
Row 53: Using MC, p9, using CC2, p6, using MC, p9.
Row 54: Using MC, k9, using CC2, k6, using MC, k9.
Row 55: Using CC1, p11, using CC2, p2, using CC1, p11.
Row 56: Using MC, k7, ssk, using CC2, k1, ssk, k2tog, k1, using MC, k2tog, k7. (*20 sts*)
Row 57: Using MC, p8, using CC2, p4, using MC, p8.
Bind (cast) off, matching yarn color for each section.

Arm/leg
(make four)
Using MC, cast on 14 sts.
Starting with a k row, work 4 rows in st st.
Row 5: Using CC1, k.
Change to MC.
Starting with a p row, work 4 rows in st st.
Row 10: Using CC1, p.
Change to MC.
Starting with a k row, work 4 rows in st st.
Row 15: Using CC1, k.
Change to CC2.
Starting with a p row, work 3 rows in st st.
Row 19: K2, M1, k4, M1, k2, M1, k4, M1, k2. (*18 sts*)
Row 20: Purl.
Row 21: K2, M1, k6, M1, k2, M1, k6, M1, k2. (*22 sts*)

60 forests and jungles

Row 22: Purl.
Row 23: K2, ssk, k4, k2tog, k2, ssk, k4, k2tog, k2. (*18 sts*)
Row 24: Purl.
Row 25: K2, ssk, k2, k2tog, k2, ssk, k2, k2tog, k2. (*14 sts*)
Row 26: Purl.
Divide rem sts evenly between two needles and, with RS tog and using third needle, bind (cast) off using three-needle bind (cast) off technique (see page 139).

Ear
(make two)
Using CC1, cast on 10 sts.
Break off CC1 and join in MC.
Row 1 (RS): Knit.
Row 2: P6, p2tog, turn. (*9 sts*)
Row 3: Sl1, k2, k2togtbl, turn. (*8 sts*)
Row 4: Sl1, p2, p2tog, turn. (*7 sts*)
Row 5: Sl1, k2, k2togtbl, turn. (*6 sts*)
Row 6: Sl1, p2, p2tog, turn. (*5 sts*)
Row 7: Sl1, k2, k2togtbl, turn. (*4 sts*)
Bind (cast) off.

Tail
Using MC, cast on 4 sts.
Row 1 (WS): Purl.
Row 2: K1, M1, k2, M1, k1. (*6 sts*)
Row 3: Purl.
Row 4: Cast on 2 sts, k to end. (*8 sts*)
Row 5: Cast on 2 sts, p to end. (*10 sts*)
Row 6: Knit.
Row 7: Purl.
Change to CC1.
Row 8: Knit.
Change to MC.
Starting with a p row, work 4 rows in st st.
Change to CC1.
Row 13: Purl.
Change to MC.
Starting with a k row, work 3 rows in st st.
Row 17: Purl.
Rep Rows 8–17 once more, then Rows 8–13 again.
Change to CC2 yarn.
Starting with a k row, work 4 rows in st st.
Row 38: [K2tog] 5 times. (*5 sts*)
Thread yarn through rem sts to fasten off.

Making up
Using matching yarn, sew the cast-on edges of the front of the muzzle together. Sew the underside of the top of the nose to the top of the muzzle, then sew the remainder of the muzzle seam underneath the chin. Fold the nose down and sew in place to the end of the CC2 section.

Stuff the head with toy filling. Add the safety eyes to the head by pushing through the knitting using the photos as a guide for position. When you are happy with the placement, remove the toy filling and firmly push the backs onto the post of each eye.

Re-stuff the head and continue sewing the seam underneath the head using matching yarn. Secure the yarn to the bottom of the head and thread the needle up to the base of one eye. Thread the needle back down to the base of the head and pull the thread, repeat for the second eye. This gives the head a more realistic shape.

Pin the ears in place on the top of the head and when you are happy with their position, sew in place.

Starting at the neck, using matching yarn, sew the seam along the back of the body. Stuff with toy filling and sew the base in place. Pin the head to the body, matching the back seams and sew in place.

Starting at the bound- (cast-) off edge of the arm/leg, sew the seam from the paw and along the limb, stuffing the paw with toy filling. Sew the cast-on edge closed. Repeat for the other three limbs. Using A, embroider three claws using straight stitches (see page 142) and pulling the yarn tight to add definition. Stuff the arms with toy filling. Using the photos for guidance, pin the arms in place with the seam underneath, and then sew firmly to the body. Sew the legs firmly in place with the seams on the inside edge of each leg.

Sew the side seam of the tail with matching yarn, stuffing with toy filling as you go. Do not stuff the end of the tail that will be sewn to the body. Pin the tail to the back of the body along the back seam then sew in place.

Using A, embroider the mouth using straight stitches, and three whiskers on each side of the face.

TIP To make it easier, I used short lengths of yarn for the black stripes. Don't worry if you end up with lots of yarn ends—they will be hidden inside the tiger once you have sewn it up.

Skill Level ★ ★ ★

snoozy the sloth

This sleepy sloth's long limbs are knitted using the i-cord
technique and finished with three claws on each arm and leg.

Yarn and materials
Rowan Felted Tweed (50% wool, 25%
viscose, 25% alpaca) light worsted (DK)
weight yarn, 191yd (175m) per 1¾oz
(50g) ball
  1 balls of Rose Quartz 206 (light
    brown) (MC)
  ¼ ball of Clay 177 (off-white) (CC1)
  Small amount of Phantom 153 (dark
    brown) (CC2)
Small amount of black fingering (4-ply)
weight yarn (A)
Pair of 5mm black domed safety eyes
Toy filling

Needles and equipment
US 2 or 3 (3mm) knitting needles
Pair of US 2 or 3 (3mm) double-pointed
needles (DPNs)
Yarn needle
Scissors
Pins

Finished size
Base to top of head: 5½in (14cm)

Gauge (tension)
Approx 26 sts to 4in (10cm) measured
over stockinette (stocking) stitch using
US 2 or 3 (3mm) knitting needles.

Abbreviations
See page 143.

Pattern note
The head of the sloth is worked in
intarsia, so wind several small balls of
the three main colors before you begin.

Body and head
Starting at base of body.
Using MC, cast on 30 sts.
Row 1 (WS): Purl.
Row 2: K7, M1, k1, M1, k3, M1, k8, M1, k3, M1, k1, M1, k7.
(*36 sts*)
Row 3: Purl.
Row 4: K8, M1, k1, M1, k5, M1, k8, M1, k5, M1, k1, M1, k8.
(*42 sts*)
Row 5: Purl.
Row 6: Knit.
Row 7: Purl.
Row 8: K9, M1, k1, M1, k7, M1, k8, M1, k7, M1, k1, M1, k9.
(*48 sts*)
Row 9: Purl.
Row 10: K10, M1, k1, M1, k9, M1, k8, M1, k9, M1, k1, M1, k10.
(*54 sts*)
Row 11: Purl.
Row 12: K23, M1, k8, M1, k23. (*56 sts*)
Starting with a p row, work 15 rows in st st.
Row 28: K10, ssk, k1, k2tog, k6, ssk, k8, k2tog, k6, ssk, k1,
k2tog, k10. (*48 sts*)
Row 29: Purl.
Row 30: K9, ssk, k1, k2tog, k4, ssk, k8, k2tog, k4, ssk, k1,
k2tog, k9. (*42 sts*)
Row 31: Purl.
Row 32: K8, ssk, k1, k2tog, k2, ssk, k8, k2tog, k2, ssk, k1,
k2tog, k8. (*36 sts*)
Next two rows create definition between body and head.
Row 33: P14, bind (cast) off 8 sts, then p13.
Row 34: K14, pick up and k 8 sts, k14. (*36 sts*)
Row 35: Purl.
Row 36: K16, M1, k4, M1, k16. (*38 sts*)

Row 37: P17, M1, p4, M1, p17. (*40 sts*)
Join in CC1 and second ball of MC and work in intarsia
(see page 141).
Row 38: Using MC, k18, using CC1, k4, using MC, k18.
Row 39: Using MC, p16, using CC1, p8, using MC, p16.
Row 40: Using MC, k14, using CC1, k12, using MC, k14.
Row 41: Using MC, p13, using CC1, p14, using MC, p13.
Row 42: Using MC, k13, using CC1, k14, using MC, k13.
Row 43: Using MC, p13, using CC1, p14, using MC, p13.
Join in two separate balls of CC.
Row 44: Using MC, k13, using CC2, k1, using CC1, k12,
using CC2, k1, using MC, k13.
Row 45: Using MC, p13, using CC2, p3, using CC1, p8,
using CC2, p3, using MC, p13.
Row 46: Using MC, k13, using CC2, k5, using CC1, k4,
using CC2, k5, using MC, k13.
Row 47: Using MC, p13, using CC2, p5, using CC1, p4,
using CC2, p5, using MC, p13.
Row 48: Using MC, k13, using CC1, k1, using CC2, k4,
using CC1, k4, using CC2, k4, using CC1 k1, using MC, k13.
Row 49: Using MC, p13, using CC1, p2, using CC2, p3,
using CC1, p4, using CC2, p2, using CC1, p2, using MC, p13.
Row 50: Using MC, k14, using CC1, k12, using MC, k14.
Row 51: Using MC, p16, using CC1, p8, using MC, p16.
Row 52: Using MC, k8, ssk, k1, k2tog, k4, using CC1, k6,
using MC, k4, ssk, k1, k2tog, k8. (*36 sts*)
Row 53: Using MC, p16, using CC1, p4, using MC, p16.
Break off CC1 and cont using MC.
Row 54: K7, ssk, k1, k2tog, k12, ssk, k1, k2tog, k7. (*32 sts*)
Row 55: Purl.
Row 56: K6, ssk, k1, k2tog, k10, ssk, k1, k2tog, k6. (*28 sts*)
Row 57: P5, p2tog, p1, p2togtbl, p8, p2tog, p1, p2togtbl, p5.
(*24 sts*)
Bind (cast) off.

62 **forests and jungles**

Arm

(make two)
Using MC, cast on 4 sts.
Row 1 (WS): Purl.
Row 2: K1, M1, k to last st, M1, k1. (*6 sts*)
Row 3: Purl.
Rep Rows 2 and 3 twice more. (*10 sts*)
Row 8: Cast on 3 sts, k to end. (*13 sts*)
Row 9: Cast on 3 sts, p to end. (*16 sts*)
Starting with a k row, work 12 rows in st st.
Shaping is done with short rows (see page 140).
Row 22: K11, turn.
Row 23: Slds, p5, turn.
Row 24: Slds, k to end.
Starting with a p row, work 15 rows in st st.
Row 40: K3, ssk, k6, k2tog, k3. (*14 sts*)
Row 41: Purl.
Row 42: K3, ssk, k4, k2tog, k3. (*12 sts*)
Row 43: Purl.
Bind (cast) off.

Leg

(make two)
Using MC, cast on 4 sts.
Row 1 (WS): Purl.
Row 2: K1, M1, k to last st, M1, k1. (*6 sts*)
Row 3: Purl.
Rep Rows 2 and 3 twice more. (*10 sts*)
Row 8: Cast on 3 sts, k to end. (*13 sts*)
Row 9: Cast on 3 sts, p to end. (*16 sts*)
Starting with a k row, work 8 rows in st st.
Shaping is done with short rows.
Row 18: K11, turn.
Row 19: Slds, p5, turn.
Row 20: Slds, k to end.
Starting with a p row, work 9 rows in st st.
Row 30: K3, ssk, k6, k2tog, k3. (*14 sts*)
Row 31: Purl.
Row 32: K3, ssk, k4, k2tog, k3. (*12 sts*)
Row 33: Purl.
Bind (cast) off.

Claw

(make three for each arm and leg)
Using CC1 and DPNs, cast on 3 sts.
Row 1: K3, push sts to other end of needle, pulling yarn firmly across back of work, without turning.
Rep Row 1 twice more.
Bind (cast) off.

Nose

Using CC2 yarn, cast on 3 sts.
Row 1 (WS): Purl.
Row 2: [K1, M1] twice, k1. (*5 sts*)
Row 3: Purl.
Row 4: Ssk, k1, k2tog. (*3 sts*)
Row 5: Purl.
Bind (cast) off.

Making up

Pin the body and head together and stuff with toy filling. Add the safety eyes to the head by pushing through the knitting using the photos as a guide for position. When you are happy with the placement, remove the toy filling and firmly push the backs onto the post of each eye. Re-stuff the head.

Starting at the top of the head, sew the seam closed across the top then continue sewing the seam down the back of the body. Stuff with toy filling as you go and sew the cast-on edges together.

Sew the nose in place to the front of the face, placing a small amount of toy filling inside to add definition. Using A, embroider the mouth using straight stitches (see page 142).

Thread the bound- (cast-) off end of yarn down the claw. Repeat for two more claws. Place the claws in a line and sew through all three close to the cast-on edges. Place the edge of the claws on top of the RS of an arm/leg, at bound- (cast-) off edge to one side—so that when the limb is folded over it will encase the sewn end of the claws. Sew the edge of the claws to the limb, taking care to stitch through the limb just above the bound- (cast-) off edge. Fold the limb over and sew to the back of the claws, so that the claws are encased. Sew the edge of the limb together and continue sewing the seam up to the top. Repeat for remaining three arms and legs.

Using the photos for guidance on position, pin the arms and legs onto the body. Sew firmly in place.

64 forests and jungles

ozzy the koala bear

Skill Level ★★★

This appealing little koala is a simple but effective knit. Did you know that koalas share more common features with kangaroos than they do with bears?

Yarn and materials
Rowan Felted Tweed (50% wool, 25% viscose, 25% alpaca) light worsted (DK) weight yarn, 191yd (175m) per 1¾oz (50g) ball
  1 ball of Scree 165 (light gray) (MC)
  Small amount of Carbon 159 (dark gray) (CC1)
Rowan Alpaca Classic (57% alpaca, 43% cotton) light worsted (DK) weight yarn, 131yd (120m) per ⅞oz (50g) ball
  ½ ball of Snowflake White 115 (CC2)
Small amount of black fingering (4-ply) yarn (A)
Toy filling
Pair of 6mm black domed safety eyes

Needles and equipment
US 2 or 3 (3mm) knitting needles
Spare knitting needle for three-needle bind (cast) off
Yarn needle
Scissors
Pins

Finished size
Top of head to toe: 8¼in (21cm)

Gauge (tension)
Approx 26 sts to 4in (10cm) measured over stockinette (stocking) stitch using US 2 or 3 (3mm) knitting needles.

Abbreviations
See page 143.

Body

Start at neck.
Using MC, cast on 32 sts.
Join in CC2 and second mini ball of MC, work in intarsia (see page 141).
Row 1: Using MC, k8, using CC2, k16, using MC, k8.
Row 2: Using MC, p8, using CC2, p16, using MC, p8.
Rep last 2 rows once more.
Row 5: Using MC, k7, M1, k1, using CC2, k1, M1, k14, M1, k1, using MC, k1, M1, k7. (*36 sts*)
Row 6: Using MC, p9, using CC2, p18, using MC, p9.
Row 7: Using MC, k9, using CC2, k18, using MC, k9.
Row 8: Using MC, p9, using CC2, p18, using MC, p9.
Row 9: Using MC, k8, M1, k1, using CC2, k1, M1, k16, M1, k1, using MC, k1, M1, k8. (*40 sts*)
Row 10: Using MC, p10, using CC2, p20, using MC, p10.
Row 11: Using MC, k10, using CC2, k20, using MC, k10.
Row 12: Using MC, p10, using CC2, p20, using MC, p10.
Row 13: Using MC, k9, M1, k1, using CC2, k1, M1, k18, M1, k1, using MC, k1, M1, k9. (*44 sts*)
Row 14: Using MC, p11, using CC2, p22, using MC, p11.
Row 15: Using MC, k10, M1, k1, using CC2, k1, M1, k20, M1, k1, using MC, k1, M1, k10. (*48 sts*)
Row 16: Using MC, p12, using CC2, p24, using MC, p12.
Row 17: Using MC, k15, using CC2, k18, using MC, k15.
Row 18: Using MC, p18, using CC2, p12, using MC, p18.
Row 19: Using MC, k21, using CC2, k6, using MC, k21.
Break off CC2 and second ball of MC, cont in MC as foll:
Starting with a p row, work 11 rows in st st.
Row 31: K8, ssk, k1, k2tog, k22, ssk, k1, k2tog, k8. (*44 sts*)
Row 32: Purl.
Row 33: K7, ssk, k1, k2tog, k20, ssk, k1, k2tog, k7. (*40 sts*)
Row 34: Purl.
Row 35: Bind (cast) off 14 sts, then k to end. (*26 sts*)
Row 36: Bind (cast) off 14 sts, then p to end. (*12 sts*)
Row 36: Knit.
Row 38: Purl.
Row 39: K2, M1, k to last 2 sts, M1, k2. (*14 sts*)
Row 40: P2, M1, p to last 2 sts, M1, p2. (*16 sts*)
Row 41: K2, M1, k to last 2 sts, M1, k2. (*18 sts*)
Starting with a p row, work 3 rows in st st.
Row 45: K2, ssk, k to last 4 sts, k2tog, k2. (*16 sts*)
Row 46: P2, p2tog, p to last 4 sts, p2togtbl, p2. (*14 sts*)
Row 47: K2, ssk, k to last 4 sts, k2tog, k2. (*12 sts*)
Bind (cast) off.

Head

Starting at base of head.
Using MC, cast on 32 sts.
Join in mini ball of CC2 and MC, cont using intarsia.
Row 1: Using MC, k13, using CC2, k6, using MC, k13.
Row 2: Using MC, p13, using CC2, p6, using MC, p13.
Row 3: Using MC, k8, M1, k5, M1, using CC2, k6, using MC, M1, k5, M1, k8. (*36 sts*)
Row 4: Using MC, p15, using CC2, p6, using MC, p15.
Row 5: Using MC, k8, M1, k1, M1, k6, using CC2, k6, using MC, k6, M1, k1, M1, k8. (*40 sts*)

Row 6: Using MC, p17, using CC2, p6, using MC, p17.
Row 7: Using MC, k9, M1, k1, M1, k7, M1, using CC2, k6, using MC, M1, k7, M1, k1, M1, k9. (*46 sts*)
Row 8: Using MC, p20, using CC2, p6, using MC, p20.
Row 9: Using MC, k10, M1, k1, M1, k9, using CC2, k6, using MC, k9, M1, k1, M1, k10. (*50 sts*)
Row 10: Using MC, p22, using CC2, p6, using MC, p22.
Row 11: Using MC, k22, using CC2, k6, using MC, k22.
Row 12: Using MC, p22, using CC2, p6, using MC, p22.
Rep last 2 rows once more.
Break off C.
Starting with a k row, work 8 rows in st st.
Row 23: K10, ssk, k1, k2tog, k20, ssk, k1, k2tog, k10. (*46 sts*)
Row 24: Purl.
Row 25: K9, ssk, k1, k2tog, k18, ssk, k1, k2tog, k9. (*42 sts*)
Row 26: Purl.
Row 27: K8, ssk, k1, k2tog, k16, ssk, k1, k2tog, k8. (*38 sts*)
Row 28: Purl.
Row 29: K7, ssk, k1, k2tog, k14, ssk, k1, k2tog, k7. (*34 sts*)
Row 30: P6, p2tog, p1, p2togtbl, p12, p2tog, p1, p2togtbl, p6. (*30 sts*)
Bind (cast) off.

Leg

(make two)
Using MC, cast on 18 sts.
Starting with a k row, work 10 rows in st st.
Row 11: K8, M1, k2, M1, k8. (*20 sts*)
Row 12: P9, M1, p2, M1, p9. (*22 sts*)
Row 13: K10, M1, k2, M1, k10. (*24 sts*)
Starting with a p row, work 3 rows in st st.
Row 17: Bind (cast) off 9 sts, then k to end. (*15 sts*)
Row 18: Bind (cast) off 9 sts, then p to end. (*6 sts*)
Row 19: Knit.
Row 20: Purl.
Row 21: K1, M1, k to last st, M1, k1. (*8 sts*)
Row 22: Purl.
Rep last 2 rows once more. (*10 sts*)
Row 25: Knit.
Row 26: Purl.
Row 27: K1, ssk, k to last 3 sts, k2tog, k1. (*8 sts*)

Row 28: Purl.
Rep last 2 rows once more. (*6 sts*)
Bind (cast) off.

Left arm
Using MC, cast on 6 sts.
Starting with a k row, work 2 rows in st st.
Row 3: K1, M1, k to last st, M1, k1. (*8 sts*)
Row 4: Purl.
Rep last 2 rows once more. (*10 sts*)
Join in CC2 and work in intarsia.
Row 7: Using CC2, cast on 8 sts, k8, using MC, k10. (*18 sts*)
Row 8: Using MC, p10, using CC2, p8.
Row 9: Using CC2, k8, using MC, k10.
Row 10: Using MC, p10, using CC2, p8.
Rep the last 2 rows seven more times.
Row 25: Using CC2, k1, ssk, k3, k2tog, using MC, ssk, k5, k2tog, k1. (*14 sts*)
Row 26: Using MC, p8, using CC2, p6.
Row 27: Using CC2, k1, ssk, k1, k2tog, using MC, ssk, k3, k2tog, k1. (*10 sts*)
Row 28: Using MC, p1, p2tog, p2togtbl, p1, using CC2, p4. (*8 sts*)
Divide rem sts evenly between two needles and, with RS tog and using third needle, bind (cast) off using three-needle bind (cast) off technique (see page 139).

Right arm
Using MC, cast on 6 sts.
Starting with a k row, work 2 rows in st st.
Row 3: K1, M1, k to last st, M1, k1. (*8 sts*)
Row 4: Purl.
Rep last 2 rows once more. (*10 sts*)
Join in CC2 and work in intarsia.
Row 7: Using MC, k10, using CC2, cast on 8 sts. (*18 sts*)
Row 8: Using CC2, p8, using MC, p10.
Row 9: Using MC, k10, using CC2, k8.
Row 10: Using CC2, p8, using MC, p10.
Rep last 2 rows seven more times.
Row 25: Using MC, k1, ssk, k5, k2tog, using CC2, ssk, k3, k2tog, k1. (*14 sts*)
Row 26: Using CC2, p6, using MC, p8.
Row 27: Using MC, k1, ssk, k3, k2tog, using CC2, ssk, k1, k2tog, k1. (*10 sts*)
Row 28: Using CC2, p4, using MC, p1, p2tog, p2togtbl, p1. (*8 sts*)
Divide rem sts evenly between two needles and, with RS tog and using third needle, bind (cast) off using three-needle bind (cast) off technique.

Ear
(make two)
Using MC, cast on 12 sts.
Starting with a k row, work 8 rows in st st.
Row 9: K1, ssk, k to last 3 sts, k2tog, k1. (*10 sts*)
Row 10: Purl.

Row 11: K1, ssk, k to last 3 sts, k2tog, k1. (*8 sts*)
Row 12: P1, p2tog, p to last 3 sts, p2togtbl, p1. (*6 sts*)
Row 13: K1, ssk, k to last 3 sts, k2tog, k1. (*4 sts*)
Row 14: Purl.
Break off MC and change to CC2.
Row 15: Knit.
Row 16: P1, M1, p to last st, M1, p1. (*6 sts*)
Row 17: K1, M1, k to last st, M1, k1. (*8 sts*)
Row 18: P1, M1, p to last st, M1, p1. (*10 sts*)
Starting with a k row, work 8 rows in st st.
Bind (cast) off.

Nose
Using CC1, cast on 3 sts.
Row 1 (WS): Purl.
Row 2: [K1, M1] twice, k1. (*5 sts*)
Row 3: P1, M1, p3, M1, p1. (*7 sts*)
Row 4: K1, M1, k5, M1, k1. (*9 sts*)
Starting with a p row, work 5 rows in st st.
Row 10: K1, ssk, k3, k2tog, k1. (*7 sts*)
Row 11: P1, p2tog, p1, p2togtbl, p1. (*5 sts*)
Row 12: Ssk, k1, k2tog. (*3 sts*)
Bind (cast) off.

Making up
Pin the head together and stuff with toy filling. Using the photos as a guide for position, pin the nose in place. Add the safety eyes to the head by pushing through the knitting using the photos as a guide for position. When you are happy with the placement, remove the stuffing and the nose and firmly push the backs onto the post of each eye. Pin the nose back in place between the eyes and add a small amount of toy filling inside for definition. Sew in place.

Sew the seam across the top of the head, then continue sewing along the back of the head stuffing with toy filling as you go. Gather the cast-on edge of the head, leaving a circle approximately ¾in (2cm) across. Add toy filling, if necessary, through this hole.

Starting at the neck, sew the seam down the back of the body. Fold the base up and sew in place. Stuff with toy filling. Sew the head firmly to the body.

Sew the side seam of the arm and stuff with toy filling. Repeat for the second arm. Pin the arms in place with the seams facing downward, using the photos for guidance, then sew in place.

Sew the seam along the leg, then fold the base of the foot up and sew in place. Stuff with toy filling. Pin the legs to the body, using the photos as a guide for position, then sew in place.

Sew the side seam on the ear closed. Repeat for the second ear. Pin the ears onto the head and when you are happy they are level, sew in place.

Using A, embroider the mouth using straight stitches (see page 142) as shown in the photo.

Skill Level ★ ★ ★

buddy the reindeer

The body of this cheerful little reindeer is started at the front and creates a little "dip" for the head to sit in, giving him a lovely look. If you prefer, you can work the nose in brown yarn or stick to red for that festive feel.

Yarn and materials
Rowan Felted Tweed (50% wool, 25% viscose, 25% alpaca) light worsted (DK) weight yarn, 191yd (175m) per 1¾oz (50g) ball

 ¾ ball of Rose Quartz 206 (light brown) (MC)

 ⅓ ball of Phantom 153 (dark brown (CC1)

Rico Ricorumi DK (100% cotton) light worsted (DK) weight yarn, 63yd (58m) per ⅞oz (25g) ball

 Small amount of Red shade 028 (CC2)

Toy filling

Pair of 5mm black domed safety eyes

Small amount of black fingering (4-ply) weight yarn (A)

Needles and equipment
US 2 or 3 (3mm) knitting needles

Spare knitting needle for three-needle bind (cast) off

Yarn needle

Scissors

Pins

Finished size
Nose to tail: 7⅛in (18cm)

Top of head to foot: 6¼in (16cm)

Gauge (tension)
Approx 26 sts to 4in (10cm) measured over stockinette (stocking) stitch using US 2 or 3 (3mm) knitting needles.

Abbreviations
See page 143.

Head
Using MC, cast on 14 sts.
Row 1 (WS): Purl.
Work inc rows as foll:
Row 2: K1, [kfb, k1, kfb] to last st, k1. (*22 sts*)
Row 3: Purl.
Row 4: K1, [kfb, k3, kfb] to last st, k1. (*30 sts*)
Row 5: Purl.
Row 6: K1, [kfb, k5, kfb] to last st, k1. (*38 sts*)
Row 7: Purl.
Starting with a k row, work 4 rows in st st.
Row 12: K1, M1, k15, ssk, k2, k2tog, k15, M1, k1.
Row 13: Purl.
Rep last two rows twice more (st count will rem the same).
Starting with a k row, work 4 rows in st st.
Row 22: K2, ssk, k to last 4 sts, k2tog, k2. (*36 sts*)
Row 23: Purl.
Rep last two rows twice more. (*32 sts*)
Row 28: K1, ssk, k to last 3 sts, k2tog, k1. (*30 sts*)
Row 29: P1, p2tog, p to last 3 sts, p2togtbl, p1. (*28 sts*)
Rep last two rows once more. (*24 sts*)
Divide rem sts evenly between two needles and, with RS tog and using third needle, bind (cast) off using three-needle bind (cast) off technique (see page 139).

> **TIP** If you would like to make this little reindeer even more festive, you could make him a mini scarf by casting on 8 sts using red yarn and knitting until it is long enough to go around his neck and keep him cozy.

buddy the reindeer 69

Body
Using MC, cast on 14 sts.
Row 1 (WS): Purl.
Row 2: K1, [kfb, k1, kfb] to last st, k1. (*22 sts*)
Row 3: Purl.
Row 4: K1, [kfb, k3, kfb] to last st, k1. (*30 sts*)
Row 5: Purl.
Row 6: K1, [kfb, k5, kfb] to last st, k1. (*38 sts*)
Row 7: Purl.
Row 8: K1, [kfb, k7, kfb] to last st, k1. (*46 sts*)
Row 9: Purl.
Row 10: K1, [kfb, k9, kfb] to last st, k1. (*54 sts*)
Row 11: Purl.
Work 6 rows in st st.
Row 18: K2, M1, k22, ssk, k2, k2tog, k22, M1, k2.
Row 19: Purl.
Rep last two rows four more times (st count will rem the same).
Work 6 rows in st st.
Row 34: K2, ssk, k to last 4 sts, k2tog, k2. (*52 sts*)
Row 35: Purl.
Rep last two rows three more times. (*46 sts*)
Row 42: K2, ssk, k to last 4 sts, k2tog, k2. (*44 sts*)
Row 43: P2, p2tog, p to last 4 sts, p2togtbl, p2. (*42 sts*)
Rep last two rows once more. (*38 sts*)
Row 46: K2, ssk, k14, M1, k2, M1, k14, k2tog, k2.
Row 47: P2, p2tog, p14, M1, p2, M1, p14, p2togtbl, p2.
Divide rem sts evenly between two needles and, with RS tog and using third needle, bind (cast) off using three-needle bind (cast) off technique.

Legs
(make four)
Using MC, cast on 12 sts.
Starting with a k row, work 10 rows in st st.
Row 11: [K2, M1] 5 times, k2. (*17 sts*)
Break off B, join in CC1.
Starting with a p row, work five rows in st st.
Row 17: Bind (cast) off 7 sts, then k to end. (*10 sts*)
Row 18: Bind (cast) off 7 sts, then p to end. (*3 sts*)
Row 19: [K1, M1] twice, k1. (*5 sts*)
Row 20: Purl.
Row 21: K1, M1, k3, M1, k1. (*7 sts*)
Starting with a p row, work 3 rows in st st.
Row 25: K1, ssk, k1, k2tog, k1. (*5 sts*)
Row 26: P2tog, p1, p2togtbl. (*3 sts*)
Bind (cast) off.

Nose
Using CC2, cast on 3 sts.
Row 1 (WS): [P1, M1] twice, p1. (*5 sts*)
Row 2: K1, M1, k3, M1, k1. (*7 sts*)
Starting with a p row, work 3 rows in st st.
Row 6: K1, ssk, k1, k2tog, k1. (*5 sts*)
Row 7: P2tog, p1, p2tog. (*3 sts*)
Thread yarn through rem sts to fasten off.

Ears
(make two)
Using MC, cast on 5 sts.
Starting with a k row, work 6 rows in st st.
Row 7: K2tog, k1, k2tog. (*3 sts*)
Starting with a p row, work 6 rows in st st.
Bind (cast) off.

Long antler piece
(make two)
Using CC1, cast on 8 sts.
Starting with a k row, work in st st until work measures 2in (5cm).
Bind (cast) off.

Short antler piece
(make four)
Using CC1, cast on 7 sts.
Starting with a k row, work in st st until work measures ¾in (2cm).
Bind (cast) off.

Making up

Starting at the bound- (cast-) off end of the body sew the seam, stuffing with toy filling as you go, ensuring the tail has enough toy filling inside. Continue sewing the seam to the front of the body, gather the cast-on edge closed and fasten off.

Pin the head together and stuff with toy filling. Add the safety eyes to the head by pushing through the knitting using the photos as a guide for position. When you are happy with the placement, remove the pins and toy filling and firmly push the backs onto the post of each eye. Re-stuff and sew the head to the front of the body.

Sew a gathering thread around the nose. Place a small amount of toy filling inside then pull the yarn to gather the nose. Using the photos for guidance, sew the nose to the front of the head.

Using MC, and starting at the top of the leg, sew the seam that will be at the back. Change to CC1 and finish sewing the seam. Stuff the foot with toy filling (leaving the leg unstuffed). Fold the base of the foot up and sew in place. Repeat for the remaining three legs. Pin the legs in place, using the photos as a guide for position and sew in place.

Fold the ear in half and sew along the side seams. The narrower part of the ear will be at the front. Fold the edges in at the bottom to give the ear a good shape and sew a few stitches to secure. Repeat for the second ear. Pin the ears in place using the photos as a guide, leaving a gap for the antlers in between. Sew the side seams of each antler piece, then sew the shorter antler pieces to the main antler following the photos. Repeat for the second antler. Pin the antlers in place between the ears and sew in place.

Using A, embroider the mouth using backstitch (see page 142).

buddy the reindeer

Skill Level ★ ★ ★

slither the scarlet king snake

This king snake is an easy knit, worked from the tip of the tail to the front of the head with simple stripes. King snakes use quick, jerky movements so that their bands flash, startling predators.

Yarn and materials
Rico Ricorumi DK (100% cotton) light worsted (DK) weight yarn, 63yd (58m) per ⅞oz (25g) ball
  1 ball of Red 028 (MC)
  ¾ ball of Black 060 (CC1)
  ¾ ball of Saffron 063 (yellow) (CC2)

Toy filling

Pair of 5mm black domed safety eyes

Needles and equipment
US 2 or 3 (3mm) knitting needles

Yarn needle

Scissors

Pins

Finished size
Length: 15¾in (40cm)

Gauge (tension)
Approx 26 sts to 4in (10cm) measured over stockinette (stocking) stitch using US 2 or 3 (3mm) knitting needles.

Abbreviations
See page 143.

Body and head
Using MC, cast on 3 sts.
Starting with a p row, work 3 rows in st st.
Row 4: [K1, M1] twice, k1. (*5 sts*)
Starting with a p row, work 3 rows in st st.
Row 8: K1, M1, k to last st, M1, k1. (*7 sts*)
Row 9: Purl.
Change to CC1.
Row 10: Knit.
Row 11: P1, M1, p to last st, M1, p1. (*9 sts*)
Change to CC2.
Row 12: Knit.
Row 13: P1, M1, p to last st, M1, p1. (*11 sts*)
Change to CC1.
Row 14: Knit.
Row 15: Purl.
Change to MC.
Row 16: Knit.
Row 17: P1, M1, p to last st, M1, p1. (*13 sts*)
Row 18: Knit.
Row 19: Purl.
Row 20: K1, M1, k to last st, M1, k1. (*15 sts*)
Row 21: Purl.
*Change to CC1.
Row 22: Knit.
Row 23: Purl.
Change to CC2.
Row 24: Knit.
Row 25: Purl.
Change to MC.
Starting with a k row, work 6 rows in st st.*
Rep from * to * seven more times.
Change to CC1.

Row 102: Knit.
Row 103: Purl.
Change to CC2.
Row 104: Knit.
Row 105: Purl.
Row 106: K4, M1, k2, M1, k3, M1, k2, M1, k4. (*19 sts*)
Row 107: Purl.
Break off CC2. Join in MC and CC1 and work in intarsia (see page 141).
Row 108: Using MC, k6, using CC1, k7, using MC, k6.
Row 109: Using MC, p6, using CC1, p7, using MC, p6.
Row 110: Using MC, k3, k2tog, k1, using CC1, ssk, k3, k2tog, using MC, k1, ssk, k3. (*15 sts*)
Row 111: Using MC, p5, using CC1, p2tog, p1, p2togtbl, using MC, p5. (*13 sts*)
Break off B, cont in MC.
Row 112: K3, ssk, k3, k2tog, k3. (*11 sts*)
Row 113: P2, p2tog, p3, p2togtbl, p2. (*9 sts*)
Bind (cast) off.

Making up
Starting at the head (bound/cast-off end of the body), pin together and stuff the head with toy filling. Add the safety eyes to the head by pushing through the knitting using the photos as a guide for position. When you are happy with the placement, remove the pins and toy filling and firmly push the backs onto the post of each eye. Re-stuff the head.

Begin sewing the bound- (cast-) off edges together so that the seam will be in the center of the base of the snake, stuffing as you go. Continue to the tail, then sew the tail end of the snake together.

72   forests and jungles

Chapter 3
oceans, rivers, and lakes

Skill Level ★ ★ ★

bubbles the flamingo

This colorful flamingo is worked using an amazing fluffy yarn.
I discovered that the wrong side of the work (purl) is much
fluffier than the right side, so all the fluffy parts are worked
using reverse stockinette (stocking) stitch. Her dangly legs
are knitted using the i-cord technique.

Yarn and materials

King Cole Moments DK (100% polyester)
light worsted (DK) weight yarn, 98yd
(90m) per 1¾oz (50g) ball
1¼ balls of Soft Pink 479 (MC)

Rico Ricorumi DK (100% cotton) light
worsted (DK) weight yarn, 63yd (58m)
per ⅞oz (25g) ball
2 balls of Fuchsia 014 (CC)
Small amounts of White 001 (A)
and Black 060 (B)

Pair of 6mm black domed safety eyes

Toy filling

Needles and equipment

US 2 or 3 (3mm) knitting needles

US 2 or 3 (3mm) double-pointed needles
(DPNs)

Stitch markers

Yarn needle

Scissors

Pins

Finished size

Tail to beak: 7⅛in (18cm)

Top of head to foot: 10⅝in (27cm)

Gauge (tension)

Approx 26 sts to 4in (10cm) measured
over stockinette (stocking) stitch using
US 2 or 3 (3mm) knitting needles and
Rico Ricorumi DK.

Abbreviations

See page 143.

Pattern note

When using MC, working in reverse
stockinette (stocking) stitch means that
the fluffier side of the yarn is on show.

Body

Start at tail.
Using MC, cast on 6 sts.
Row 1 (RS): Purl.
Row 2: K1, M1, k to last st, M1, k1. (*8 sts*)
Row 3: Purl.
Shaping is done with short rows (see page 140).
Row 4: K1, M1, k2, turn.
Row 5: Slds, p to end.
Row 6: K to last st, M1, k1.
Row 7: P4, turn.
Row 8: Slds, k to end. (*11 sts*)
Row 9: Purl.
Row 10: K1, M1, k2, turn.
Row 11: Slds, p to end.
Row 12: K1, M1, k4, M1, k1, M1, k4, M1, k1. (*15 sts*)
Row 13: P1, M1, p2, turn.
Row 14: Slds, k to end. (*16 sts*)
Row 15: P7, PM, p2, PM, p7.
Row 16: K1, M1, k to marker, M1, SM, k2, SM, M1, k to last st, M1, k1.
(*20 sts*)
Row 17: Purl.
Rep Rows 16 and 17 three more times. (*32 sts*)
Row 24: K1, M1, k26, turn. (*33 sts*)
Row 25: Slds, p21, turn.
Row 26: Slds, k18, turn.
Row 27: Slds, p15, turn.
Row 28: Slds, k to last st, M1, k1. (*34 sts*)
Row 29: K1, M1, k to marker, M1, SM, k2, SM, M1, k to last st, M1, k1.
(*38 sts*)
Row 30: Purl.
Rep Rows 29 and 30 once more. (*42 sts*)
Row 33: K37, turn.
Row 34: Slds, p31, turn.
Row 35: Slds, k27, turn.
Row 36: Slds, p23, turn.
Row 37: Slds, k to end.
Starting with a p row, work 7 rows in st st.
Row 45: K1, ssk, k to 2 sts before marker, ssk, SM, k2, SM, k2tog,
k to last 3 sts, k2tog, k1. (*38 sts*)
Row 46: Purl.

76 **oceans, rivers, and lakes**

Row 47: K1, ssk, k to 2 sts before marker, ssk, SM, k2, SM, k2tog, k to last 3 sts, k2tog, k1. (*34 sts*)
Row 48: P1, p2tog, p to 2 sts before marker, p2tog, SM, p2, SM, p2togtbl, p to last 3 sts, p2togtbl, p1. (*30 sts*)
Rep Rows 47 and 48 once more. (*22 sts*)
Row 51: K1, ssk, k to 2 sts before marker, ssk, SM, k2, SM, k2tog, k to last 3 sts, k2tog, k1. (*18 sts*)
Divide rem sts evenly between two needles and, with RS tog and using third needle, bind (cast) off using three-needle bind (cast) off technique (see page 139).

Neck, head, and beak

Start at bottom of neck.
Using MC, cast on 14 sts.
Starting with a p row, work 2 rows in reverse st st.
Break off MC, change to CC.
Next row will be worked on RS.
Shaping is done with short rows.
*Row 3 (RS): K6, turn.
Row 4 (WS): Slds, p to end.
Row 5: K5, turn.
Row 6: Slds, p to end.
Row 7: K4, turn.
Row 8: Slds, p to end.
Row 9: Knit.
Row 10: P6, turn.
Row 11: Slds, k to end.
Row 12: P5, turn.
Row 13: Slds, k to end.
Row 14: P4, turn.
Row 15: Slds, k to end.
Row 16: Purl.*
Starting with a k row, work 4 rows in st st.
Work from * to * once more.
**Row 35: K11, turn.
Row 36: Slds, p7, turn.
Row 37: Slds, k5, turn.
Row 38: Slds, p3, turn.
Row 39: Slds, k to end.
Row 40: Purl.**
Work from ** to ** once more.
Row 47: K1, M1, k10, turn. (*15 sts*)

> **TIP** When you make the knotty knees, make a loose knot in each leg. Place the legs side by side and slowly tighten each knot. This will help you make the knots level.

Row 48: Slds, p8, turn.
Row 49: Slds, k6, turn.
Row 50: Slds, p4, turn.
Row 51: Slds, k to last st, M1, k1. (*16 sts*)
Row 52: Purl.
Row 53: K13, turn.
Row 54: Slds, p9, turn.
Row 55: Slds, k7, turn.
Row 56: Slds, p5, turn.
Row 57: Slds, k to end.
Row 58: Purl.
Row 59: K6, k2tog, ssk, k3, turn. (*14 sts*)
Row 60: Slds, p7, turn.
Row 61: Slds, k1, k2tog, ssk, k1, turn. (*12 sts*)
Row 62: Slds, p3, turn.
Row 63: Slds, k to end.
Break off CC, change to A.
Row 64: Purl.
Row 65: K4, k2tog, ssk, k1, turn. (*10 sts*)
Row 66: Slds, p3, turn.
Row 67: Slds, k to end.
Row 68: Purl.
Row 69: K3, k2tog, ssk, k3. (*8 sts*)
Break off A, change to B.
Row 70: Purl.
Row 71: K2, k2tog, ssk, k2. (*6 sts*)
Row 72: P1, p2togtbl, p2tog, p1. (*4 sts*)
Row 73: K2tog, ssk. (*2 sts*)
Thread yarn through rem sts to fasten off, leaving length of yarn for sewing up.

Wing

(make 2)
Using MC, cast on 7 sts.
Row 1 (RS): Purl.
Row 2: K1, M1, k to last st, M1, k1. (*9 sts*)
Row 3: Purl.
Rep Rows 2 and 3 twice more. (*13 sts*)
Row 8: K2, [M1, k3] 3 times, M1, k2. (*17 sts*)
Row 9: Purl.
Row 10: K1, [M1, k3] 5 times, M1, k2. (*23 sts*)
Row 11: Purl.
Shaping is done with short rows.
Row 12: K18, turn.
Row 13: Slds, p12, turn.
Row 14: Slds, k to end.
Starting with a p row, work 7 rows in st st.
Row 22: K1, k2tog, k to last 3 sts, ssk, k1. (*21 sts*)
Row 23: Purl.
Rep Rows 22 and 23 twice more. (*17 sts*)
Bind (cast) off.

78 **oceans, rivers, and lakes**

Leg
(make 2)

Using CC and DPNs, cast on 4 sts.
Row 1: K4, push sts to other end of needle, pulling yarn firmly across back of work, without turning.
Rep Row 1 until work measures 5½in (14cm).
Beg working flat.
Next row (RS): K1, M1, k to last st, M1, k1. (*6 sts*)
Next row: Purl.
Rep last 2 rows twice more. (*10 sts*)
Starting with a k row, work 2 rows in st st.
Next row: Purl (creates fold line).
Starting with a p row, work 3 rows in st st.
Next row: K1, k2tog, k to last 3 sts, ssk, k1. (*8 sts*)
Next row: Purl.
Rep last 2 rows once more. (*6 sts*)
Next row: K1, k2tog, ssk, k1. (*4 sts*)
Next row: P2tog, p2togtbl. (*2 sts*)
Thread yarn through rem sts to fasten off, leaving length of yarn for sewing up.

Making up

Since it is a smooth yarn, it will be easier to use CC to make up.

Sew the tail seam closed and then continue sewing the seam that will be underneath the flamingo, adding toy filling as you go.

Push the safety eyes through the knitting on the head using the photos for guidance. When you are happy with their placement, push the backs firmly onto the eye posts. Starting at the cast-on edge, sew the seam that will run underneath the neck, stuffing with toy filling as you go to give the neck and head definition. Change to A and sew the beak seam, stuffing with toy filling as you go and changing to B for the tip of the beak. Using the photos for guidance, pin the neck and head to the body, then sew firmly in place using matching yarn.

Sew the ends of yarn in on each wing and pin both wings in place on either side of the body, making sure they are level. Sew the front edge of one wing to the body from the middle of the bottom edge to the top of the wing, leaving the rest of the wing unsewn. Repeat for the second wing.

Fold the bottom of the foot upward at purl ridge and sew the side seams, stuffing with a small amount of toy filling to add definition. Repeat for the second leg. Knot each leg loosely, tightening and adjusting as necessary to get both the knots level. Using the photos for guidance, sew the legs in place to the base of the body.

bubbles the flamingo

Skill Level ★ ★ ★

chilly the polar bear

This cheerful little polar bear is worked in reverse stockinette (stocking) stitch, so the purl side is on the outside, which together with the super-soft yarn makes him extra cuddly.

Yarn and materials
Rowan Alpaca Classic (57% alpaca, 43% cotton) light worsted (DK) weight yarn, 131yd (120m) per ⅞oz (50g) ball
  1 ball of Snowflake White 115

Small amount of black fingering (4-ply) weight yarn (A)

Pair of 6mm black domed safety eyes

Toy filling

Needles and equipment
US 2 or 3 (3mm) knitting needles

Spare knitting needle for three-needle bind (cast) off

Yarn needle

Scissors

Pins

Finished size
Base to top of head: 6¼in (16cm)

Gauge (tension)
Approx 26 sts to 4in (10cm) measured over stockinette (stocking) stitch using US 2 or 3 (3mm) knitting needles.

Abbreviations
See page 143.

Head
Start at nose.
Work in reverse st st.
Cast on 12 sts.
Row 1 (RS): Purl.
Row 2: K1, M1, k to last st, M1, k1. (*14 sts*)
Row 3: P1, M1, p to last st, M1, p1. (*16 sts*)
Rep Rows 2 and 3 once more. (*20 sts*)
Row 6: K1, M1, k to last st, M1, k1. (*22 sts*)
Row 7: Purl.
Bind (cast) off.
With RS facing, pick up and k 22 sts from bound- (cast-) off edge.
Cont working in reverse st st.
Row 1: K4, M1, [k2, M1] 3 times, k2, [M1, k2] 3 times, M1, k4. (*30 sts*)
Starting with a p row, work 3 rows in st st.
Row 5: K5, [M1, k5] 4 times, M1, k5. (*35 sts*)
Starting with a p row, work 3 rows in st st.
Row 9: [K6, M1] 5 times, k5. (*40 sts*)
Row 10: Purl.
Row 11: [K4, M1] 4 times, k3, M1, k2, M1, k3, [M1, k4] 4 times. (*50 sts*)
Starting with a p row, work 5 rows in st st.
Row 17: K4, ssk, [k3, ssk] 3 times, k8, [k2tog, k3] 3 times, k2tog, k4. (*42 sts*)
Row 18: Purl.
Row 19: [K3, ssk] 4 times, k2, [k2tog, k3] 4 times. (*34 sts*)
Row 20: Purl.
Row 21: [K2, ssk] 4 times, k2, [k2tog, k2] 4 times. (*26 sts*)
Row 22: Purl.
Row 23: K3, [k1, ssk] 3 times, k2, [k1, k2tog] 3 times, k3. (*20 sts*)
Row 24: Purl.
Divide rem sts evenly between two needles and, with RS tog and using third needle, bind (cast) off using three-needle bind (cast) off technique (see page 139).

Body
Start at neck.
Work in reverse st st.
Cast on 40 sts.
Starting with a k row, work 14 rows in reverse st st.
Row 15 (WS): K9, M1, k2, M1, k18, M1, k2, M1, k9. (*44 sts*)
Starting with a p row, work 3 rows in reverse st st.

80   oceans, rivers, and lakes

Row 19: K10, M1, k2, M1, k20, M1, k2, M1, k10. (*48 sts*)
Starting with a p row, work 3 rows in reverse st st.
Row 23: K23, M1, k2, M1, k23. (*50 sts*)
Row 24: Purl.
Row 25: K23, M1, k4, M1, k23. (*52 sts*)
Row 26: Purl.
Row 27: K23, M1, k6, M1, k23. (*54 sts*)
Starting with a p row, work 9 rows in reverse st st.
Row 37: K10, ssk, k2, k2tog, k22, ssk, k2, k2tog, k10. (*50 sts*)
Row 38: Purl.
Cont working in reverse st st and bind (cast) off 19 sts at beg of next two rows. (*12 sts*)
Make base.
Row 41: K2, M1, k to last 2 sts, M1, k2. (*14 sts*)
Row 42: Purl.
Rep Rows 41 and 42 three more times. (*20 sts*)
Starting with a k row, work 8 rows in reverse st st.
Row 57: K2, ssk, k to last 4 sts, k2tog, k2. (*18 sts*)
Row 58: Purl.
Rep Rows 57 and 58 once more. (*16 sts*)
Row 61: K2, ssk, k to last 4 sts, k2tog, k2. (*14 sts*)
Row 62: P2, p2togtbl, p to last 4 sts, p2tog, p2. (*12 sts*)
Bind (cast) off.

Left leg and foot
Work in reverse st st.
Cast on 6 sts.
Row 1 (RS): Purl.
Row 2: K1, M1, k to last st, M1, k1. (*8 sts*)
Row 3: Purl.
Rep Rows 2 and 3 once more. (*10 sts*)
Cast on 1 st at beg of next row, k to end. (*11 sts*)
Cast on 7 sts at beg of next row, p to end. (*18 sts*)
*Starting with a k row, work 4 rows in reverse st st.
Row 12: K8, M1, k2, M1, k8. (*20 sts*)
Row 13: P9, M1, p2, M1, p9. (*22 sts*)
Row 14: K10, M1, k2, M1, k10. (*24 sts*)
Row 15: P11, M1, p2, M1, p11. (*26 sts*)
Row 16: K12, M1, k2, M1, k12. (*28 sts*)
Row 17: P13, M1, p2, M1, p13. (*30 sts*)
Starting with a k row, work 2 rows in st st.
Cont working in reverse st st and bind (cast) off 13 sts at beg of next 2 rows. (*4 sts*)
Row 22: Knit.
Row 23: P1, M1, p to last st, M1, p1. (*6 sts*)
Row 24: K1, M1, k to last st, M1, k1. (*8 sts*)
Row 25: P1, M1, p to last st, M1, p1. (*10 sts*)
Starting with a k row, work 4 rows in st st.
Row 30: K1, ssk, k4, k2tog, k1. (*8 sts*)
Row 31: P1, p2togtbl, p2, p2tog, p1. (*6 sts*)
Row 32: K1, ssk, k2tog, k1. (*4 sts*)
Row 33: Purl.
Bind (cast) off.
Thread yarn through rem sts to fasten off, leaving length of yarn for sewing up.*

Right leg and foot
Work in reverse st st.
Cast on 6 sts.
Row 1 (RS): Purl.
Row 2: K1, M1, k to last st, M1, k1. (*8 sts*)
Row 3: Purl.
Rep Rows 2 and 3 once more. (*10 sts*)
Cast on 7 sts at beg of next row, k to end. (*17 sts*)
Cast on 1 st at beg of next row, p to end. (*18 sts*)
Work as for left leg and foot from * to *.

Left arm
Work in reverse st st.
Cast on 4 sts.
Row 1 (WS): Knit.
Row 2: P1, M1, p to last st, M1, p1. (*6 sts*)
Row 3: Knit.
Rep Rows 2 and 3 once more. (*8 sts*)
Cast on 8 sts at beg of next row, p to end. (*16 sts*)
Starting with a k row, work 8 rows in reverse st st.
Shaping is done with short rows (see page 140).
Row 15: K4, turn.
Row 16: Slds, p to end.
Row 17: K3, turn.
Row 18: Slds, p to end.
Row 19: Knit.
Row 20: P4, turn.

82 **oceans, rivers, and lakes**

Row 21: Slds, k to end.
Row 22: P3, turn.
Row 23: Slds, k to end.
Starting with a p row, work 9 rows in st st.
Row 33: K1, ssk, k3, k2tog, k1, ssk, k3, k2tog. (*12 sts*)
Row 34: Purl.
Row 35: K1, ssk, k1, k2tog, k1, ssk, k1, k2tog. (*8 sts*)
Divide rem sts evenly between two needles and, with RS tog and using third needle, bind (cast) off using three-needle bind (cast) off technique.

Right arm
Work in reverse st st.
Cast on 4 sts.
Row 1 (RS): Purl.
Row 2: K1, M1, k to last st, M1, k1. (*6 sts*)
Row 3: Purl.
Rep Rows 2 and 3 once more. (*8 sts*)
Cast on 8 sts at beg of next row, k to end. (*16 sts*)
Starting with a p row, work 8 rows in st st.
Shaping is done with short rows.
Row 15: P4, turn.
Row 16: Slds, k to end.
Row 17: Slds, p3, turn.
Row 18: Slds, k to end.
Row 19: Purl.
Row 20: K4, turn.
Row 21: Slds, p to end.
Row 22: Slds, k3, turn.
Row 23: Slds, p to end.
Starting with a k row, work 8 rows in reverse st st.
Row 32: Ssk, k3, k2tog, k1, ssk, k3, k2tog, k1. (*12 sts*)
Row 33: Purl.
Row 34: Ssk, k1, k2tog, k1, ssk, k1, k2tog, k1. (*8 sts*)
Divide rem sts evenly between two needles and, with RS tog and using third needle, bind (cast) off using three-needle bind (cast) off technique.

Ear
(make two)
Work in reverse st st.
Cast on 5 sts.
Starting with a k row, work 2 rows in st st.
Row 3: K4, turn.
Row 4: Slds, p2, turn.
Row 5: Slds, k to end.
Starting with a p row, work 3 rows in st st.
Bind (cast) off, leaving length of yarn for sewing up.

Nose
Using A, cast on 5 sts.
Starting with a k row, work 2 rows in st st.
Row 3: Ssk, k1, k2tog.
Row 4: CDD.
Thread yarn through rem st to fasten off, leaving length of yarn for sewing up.

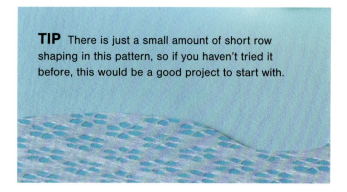

TIP There is just a small amount of short row shaping in this pattern, so if you haven't tried it before, this would be a good project to start with.

Making up
Add the safety eyes to the head by pushing through the knitting above the nose, using the photos as a guide for position. When you are happy with the placement, firmly push the backs onto the post of each eye.

Starting at the neck, sew the seam at the back of the body. Fold the base up and sew in place. Stuff with toy filling.

Stuff the head with toy filling and then pin to the top of the body, matching the back seams. When you are happy with the placement, sew firmly in place.

Sew the side seam on the arm and stuff with toy filling. Repeat for second arm. Pin the arms in place with the seams facing downward, using the photos as a guide for position, then sew in place.

Sew the seam along the leg, fold the base of the foot up and sew in place. Stuff with toy filling. Pin the legs to the body, using the photos as a guide, then sew in place.

Fold the ears in half and sew the seam closed and, as you sew pull the ears into a rounded shape. Pin the ears to the top of the head and then sew in place.

Pin in the nose to the front of the snout, placing a tiny amount of toy filling inside, and then sew in place. Using A, embroider the mouth using straight stitches (see page 142).

Skill Level ★ ★ ★

waddle the penguin

This dapper chap has an interesting construction, with the wings "sandwiched" between the bottom of the head and the body. Did you know that a group of penguins in the water is called a raft but on land they're called a waddle?

Yarn and materials

Rico Ricorumi Spray DK (100% cotton) light worsted (DK) weight yarn, 62yd (57.5m) per ⅞oz (25g) ball
  1 ball of Gray 010 (CC1)

Rico Ricorumi DK (100% cotton) light worsted (DK) weight yarn, 63yd (58m) per ⅞oz (25g) ball
  1 ball of Black 060 (MC)
  ¾ ball of White 001 (CC2)
  Small amount of Orange 027 (CC3)

Pair of 5mm black domed safety eyes

Toy filling

Needles and equipment

US 2 or 3 (3mm) knitting needles

Spare knitting needle for three-needle bind (cast) off

Yarn needle

Scissors

Pins

Finished size

Base to top of head: 5½in (14cm)

Gauge (tension)

Approx 26 sts to 4in (10cm) measured over stockinette (stocking) stitch using US 2 or 3 (3mm) knitting needles.

Abbreviations

See page 143.

Pattern note

Wind separate small balls of MC and CC2 before you begin, for the intarsia section on the body and head.

Body and head

Start at bottom of body.

Using CC1, cast on 16 sts.

Row 1: K2, M1, k to last 2 sts, M1, k2. (*18 sts*)

Row 2: Purl.

Rep last 2 rows once more. (*20 sts*)

Starting with a k row, work 14 rows in st st.

Row 19: K2, ssk, k to last 4 sts, k2tog, k2. (*18 sts*)

Starting with a p row, work 3 rows in st st.

Rep last 4 rows once more. (*16 sts*)

Row 27: K2, ssk, k to last 4 sts, k2tog, k2. (*14 sts*)

Row 28: Purl.

Break off CC1 yarn and join in MC yarn and work in intarsia (see page 141).

Row 29: Using MC, cast on 14 sts, working across these sts, k16, join in CC2 yarn, k10, join in second mini ball of MC, k2. (*28 sts*)

Row 30: Using MC, cast on 14 sts, working across these sts, p15, using CC2, p12, using MC, p15. (*42 sts*)

Row 31: Using MC, k14, using CC2, k14, using MC, k14.

Row 32: Using MC, p13, using CC2, p16, using MC, p13.

Row 33: Using MC, k13, using CC2, k16, using MC, k13.

Join in second strand of MC.

Row 34: Using MC, p13, using CC2, p6, using MC, p4, using CC2, p6, using MC, p13.

Row 35: Using MC, k2, k2tog, k9, using CC2, k6, using MC, k4, using CC2, k6, using MC, k9, k2tog, k2. (*40 sts*)

Row 36: Using MC, p13, using CC2, p5, using MC, p4, using CC2, p5, using MC, p13.

Row 37: Using MC, k14, using CC2, k4, using MC, k4, using CC2, k4, using MC, k14.

Row 38: Using MC, p15, using CC2, p2, using MC, p6, using CC2, p2, using MC, p15.

Break off CC2, cont in MC.

Row 39: K7, ssk, k2tog, k18, ssk, k2tog, k7. (*36 sts*)

84   oceans, rivers, and lakes

Starting with a p row, work 3 rows in st st.
Row 43: K6, ssk, k2tog, k16, ssk, k2tog, k6. (*32 sts*)
Row 44: Purl.
Row 45: K5, ssk, k2tog, k14, ssk, k2tog, k5. (*28 sts*)
Row 46: P4, p2tog, p2togtbl, p12, p2tog, p2togtbl, p4. (*24 sts*)
Bind (cast) off, leaving a length of yarn for sewing up.

Back
Using CC1, cast on 28 sts.
Starting with a k row, work 6 rows in st st.
Row 7: K2, M1, k to last 2 sts, M1, k2. (*30 sts*)
Row 8: Purl.
Row 9: K2, M1, k to last 2 sts, M1, k2. (*32 sts*)
Starting with a p row, work 3 rows in st st.
Rep last 4 rows once more. (*34 sts*)
Starting with a k row, work 10 rows in st st.
Row 27: K2, ssk, k to last 4 sts, k2tog, k2. (*32 sts*)
Row 28: Purl.
Row 29: Bind (cast) off 11 sts, k to end. (*21 sts*)
Row 30: Bind (cast) off 11 sts, p to end. (*10 sts*)
Starting with a k row, work 4 rows in st st.
Row 35: K2, M1, k to last 2 sts, M1, k2. (*12 sts*)
Starting with a p row, work 3 rows in st st.
Row 39: K2, M1, k to last 2 sts, M1, k2. (*14 sts*)
Row 40: Purl.
Bind (cast) off.

Wing
(make two)
Using CC1, cast on 10 sts.
Starting with a k row, work 18 rows in st st.
Row 19: K1, ssk, k to last 3 sts, k2tog, k1. (*8 sts*)
Row 20: Purl.
Rep last 2 rows three more times. (*4 sts*)
Row 27: K1, M1, k to last st, M1, k1. (*6 sts*)
Row 28: Purl.
Rep last 2 rows once more. (*8 sts*)
Starting with a k row, work 16 rows in st st.
Bind (cast) off, leaving length of yarn for sewing up.

Foot
(make two)
Using MC, cast on 6 sts.
Starting with a k row, work 12 rows in st st.
Bind (cast) off, leaving length of yarn for sewing up.

Beak
Using CC3, cast on 5 sts.
Starting with a p row, work 3 rows in st st.
Row 4: Ssk, k1, k2tog. (*3 sts*)
Row 5: Purl.
Row 6: [K1, M1] twice. (*5 sts*)
Starting with a p row, work 3 rows in st st.
Bind (cast) off.

Making up
Using matching yarn, sew the head together and stuff with toy filling. Fold the beak in half WS together and sew side seams. Using the photos as a guide for position, pin the beak in place. Push the safety eyes through the knitting and, when you are happy with their placement, remove the toy filling and firmly push the back onto the post of each eye. Re-stuff the head. Sew the beak in place.

Fold a wing in half with WS together. The narrower section is the inside of the wing. Sew the side seams; the inside of the wing will be slightly shorter than the outside. Repeat for second wing and pin both wings in place along the bottom edge of the head. Sew in place.

Pin the top edge of the back to the head, with the wings sandwiched in between. Sew in place, making sure the wings are sewn to both the head and the back of the body.

Sew the side seams of the body, stuffing with toy filling as you go.

Fold a foot in half with WS together and sew each side seam. Repeat for the second foot. Pin the feet to the lower edge of the front of the body and then sew. Fold the base up, making sure there is sufficient toy filling in the body, and sew in place, making sure the feet are caught in the seam.

86   oceans, rivers, and lakes

snapper the crocodile

Skill Level ★★★

The chunky little crocodile is knitted in one piece from her nose to the tip of her tail. The pattern along her back is knitted using little bobbles and twisted stitches, and her nostrils are also little bobbles.

Yarn and materials
Rico Ricorumi DK (100% cotton) light worsted (DK) weight yarn, 63yd (58m) per ⅞oz (25g) ball
　1½ balls of Olive 048 (green) (MC)
Small amount of White 001
Pair of 6mm black domed safety eyes
Toy filling

Needles and equipment
US 2 or 3 (3mm) knitting needles
Stitch markers
Yarn needle
Scissors
Pins

Finished size
Nose to tail: 11in (28cm)

Gauge (tension)
Approx 26 sts to 4in (10cm) measured over stockinette (stocking) stitch using US 2 or 3 (3mm) knitting needles.

Abbreviations
See page 143.

Special abbreviations
MB (make bobble): Kfb, turn, p2, turn, k2, slip second st from end of needle over first st. *(1 st)*
T2F (twist 2 front): K second stitch on LH needle, without removing st from needle, k first st on LH needle, slip both sts to RH needle. This will produce a twist to the right.
T2B (twist 2 back): K second st on LH needle through back loop, without removing st from needle, k first st on LH needle, slip both sts to RH needle. This will produce a twist to the left.

Tail and body
Start at tail.
Using MC, cast on 9 sts.
Starting with a p row, work 3 rows in st st.
Row 4 (RS): K1, M1, k3, MB, k3, M1, k1. (*11 sts*)
Starting with a p row, work 3 rows in st st.
Row 8: K2, M1, k3, MB, k3, M1, k2. (*13 sts*)
Starting with a p row, work 3 rows in st st.
Row 12: K2, M1, k4, MB, k4, M1, k2. (*15 sts*)
Starting with a p row, work 3 rows in st st.
Row 16: K3, M1, k4, MB, k4, M1, k3. (*17 sts*)
Starting with a p row, work 3 rows in st st.
Row 20: K4, M1, k4, MB, k4, M1, k4. (*19 sts*)
Starting with a p row, work 3 rows in st st.
Row 24: K4, M1, k5, MB, k5, M1, k4. (*21 sts*)
Starting with a p row, work 3 rows in st st.
Row 28: K5, M1, k5, MB, k5, M1, k5. (*23 sts*)
Starting with a p row, work 3 rows in st st.
Row 32: K5, M1, k6, MB, k6, M1, k5. (*25 sts*)
Starting with a p row, work 3 rows in st st.
Row 36: K6, M1, k6, M1, MB, M1, k6, M1, k6. (*29 sts*)
Row 37: Purl.
Row 38: K6, M1, k17, M1, k6. (*31 sts*)
Row 39: Purl.
Row 40: K6, M1, k6, M1, k1, MB, k3, MB, k1, M1, k6, M1, k6. (*35 sts*)
Row 41: Purl.
Row 42: K6, M1, k7, M1, k4, k2tog, k3, M1, k7, M1, k6. (*38 sts*)
Row 43: Purl.
Row 44: K6, M1, k10, MB, T2F, T2B, MB, k10, M1, k6. (*40 sts*)
Row 45: Purl.
Row 46: K18, T2F, T2B, k18.
Row 47: Purl.
Row 48: K17, MB, T2F, T2B, MB, k17.
Row 49: Purl.
Rep last 4 rows three more times.
Row 62: K2, ssk, k5, ssk, k4, ssk, k1, T2F, T2B, k1, k2tog, k4, k2tog, k5, k2tog, k2. (*34 sts*)
Row 63: Purl.
Row 64: K2, ssk, k3, ssk, k3, ssk, MB, T2F, T2B, MB, k2tog, k3, k2tog, k3, k2tog, k2. (*28 sts*)
Row 65: Purl.
Row 66: K10, M1, k8, M1, k10. (*30 sts*)
Row 67: P11, M1, p8, M1, p11. (*32 sts*)
Row 68: K12, M1, k8, M1, k12. (*34 sts*)
Row 69: P13, M1, p8, M1, p13. (*36 sts*)
Shaping is done with short rows (see page 140).
Row 70: K22, turn.
Row 71: Slds, p7, turn.
Row 72: Slds, k to end.
Row 73: P24, turn.
Row 74: Slds, k3, turn.
Row 75: Slds, p to end.
Row 76: K12, k2tog, k8, ssk, k12. (*34 sts*)
Row 77: P11, p2tog, p8, p2togtbl, p11. (*32 sts*)
Row 78: K10, k2tog, k8, ssk, k10. (*30 sts*)
Row 79: P9, p2tog, p8, p2togtbl, p9. (*28 sts*)
Row 80: K8, k2tog, k8, ssk, k8. (*26 sts*)
Row 81: P7, p2tog, p8, p2togtbl, p7. (*24 sts*)
Starting with a k row, work 14 rows in st st.
Row 96: K4, ssk, k2tog, k2, MB, k2, MB, k2, ssk, k2tog, k4. (*20 sts*)
Row 97: Purl.
Row 98: K3, ssk, k2tog, k6, ssk, k2tog, k3. (*16 sts*)

88　oceans, rivers, and lakes

Row 99: P2, p2tog, p2togtbl, p4, p2tog, p2togtbl, p2. (*12 sts*)
Bind (cast) off.

Right leg
Using MC, cast on 7 sts.
Row 1 (WS): Purl.
Row 2: K1, M1, k2, M1, k1, M1, k2, M1, k1. (*11 sts*).
Starting with a p row, work 3 rows in st st.
Shaping is done with short rows.
Row 6: Bind (cast) off 4 sts, then k5, turn.
Row 7: Slds, p4, turn.
Row 8: Slds, k3, turn.
Row 9: Slds, p2, turn.
Row 10: Slds, k to end. (*7 sts*)
Row 11: Purl.
Row 12: Cast on 4 sts, working across these sts k to end. (*11 sts*)
Row 13: Purl.
Row 14: K2, M1, k6, M1, k3. (*13 sts*)
Starting with a p row, work 3 rows in st st.
Row 18: [K1, k2tog] four times, k1. (*9 sts*)
Row 19: Purl.
Row 20: [K2tog] four times, k1. (*5 sts*)
Thread yarn through rem sts to fasten off, leaving length of yarn for sewing up.

Left leg
Using MC, cast on 7 sts.
Row 1 (RS): Knit.
Row 2: P1, M1, p2, M1, p1, M1, p2, M1, p1. (*11 sts*)
Starting with a k row, work 3 rows in st st.
Shaping is done with short rows.
Row 6: Bind (cast) off 4 sts, then p5, turn.
Row 7: Slds, k4, turn.
Row 8: Slds, p3, turn.
Row 9: Slds, k2, turn.
Row 10: Slds, p to end. (*7 sts*)
Row 11: Knit.
Row 12: Cast on 4 sts, working across these sts p to end. (*11 sts*)
Row 13: Knit.
Row 14: P2, M1, p6, M1, p3. (*13 sts*)
Starting with a k row, work 3 rows in st st.
Row 18: [P1, p2tog] four times, p1. (*9 sts*)
Row 19: Knit.
Row 20: [P2tog] four times, p1. (*5 sts*)
Thread yarn through rem sts to fasten off, leaving a length of yarn for sewing up.

Eyebrow
(make 2)
Using MC, cast on 6 sts.
Shaping is done with short rows.
Row 1: K5, turn.
Row 2: Slds, p3, turn.
Row 3: Slds, k to end.
Row 4: Purl.
Bind (cast) off, leaving a length of yarn for sewing up.

Making up
On the tail and body sew the cast-on edge together so that the body seam will be underneath the crocodile. Sew the body seam up to the head, stuffing with toy filling as you go. Pin the seam together underneath the head and stuff the head with toy filling. Using the photos as a guide for position, push the safety eyes through the knitting. With the bound- (cast-) off edge of an eyebrow close to the eye, pin in place so that it curls around the eye. Sew the bound- (cast-) off edge in place and then the cast on edge. Repeat for the second eye. Remove as much toy filling as you can and firmly push the back onto the post of each eye. Re-stuff the head and continue sewing the seam to the bound- (cast-) off edge. Sew the bound- (cast-) off edge together, ensuring the bound- (cast-) off stitches are inside the seam, leaving a neat result.

Fold the foot in half and sew the seam around the edges. Joining cast-on/bound- (cast-) off edges forms top of ankle. Fill with toy filling, making sure to push it into the heel of the foot. Starting at the bound- (cast-) off edge, gather the stitches and sew the seam along the side of the leg, stuffing with toy filling as you go. Lift the foot and sew to the leg so that the foot is at a 90-degree angle to the leg. Repeat for the remaining three legs. Pin each leg in place, using the photos as a guide for position and then sew in place.

Using A, embroider the teeth using straight stitches (see page 142).

snapper the crocodile

Skill Level ★ ★ ★

splashy the whale

This rotund little whale is knitted from the top of his head, with the bound- (cast-) off edge forming his belly. Did you know that blue whales are bigger than dinosaurs?

Yarn and materials
Rico Ricorumi DK (100% cotton) light worsted (DK) weight yarn, 63yd (58m) per ⅞oz (25g) ball
    2 balls of Midnight Blue 035 (MC)
    1¼ balls of Light Blue 033 (CC)
Small amount of black fingering (4-ply) weight yarn
Pair of 5mm black domed safety eyes
Toy filling

Needles and equipment
US 2 or 3 (3mm) knitting needles
Two spare knitting needles
Yarn needle
Scissors
Pins

Finished size
Nose to tip of tail: 7⅛in (18cm)
Base to top of head: 4¼in (11cm)

Gauge (tension)
Approx 26 sts to 4in (10cm) measured over stockinette (stocking) stitch using US 2 or 3 (3mm) knitting needles.

Abbreviations
See page 143.

Pattern note
Wind separate small balls of MC and CC before you begin, for the intarsia sections on the head and body.

Top of fin
(make 2)
Using MC, cast on 4 sts.
Row 1 (WS): Purl.
Row 2: K1, M1, k2, M1, k1. (*6 sts*)
Row 3: P1, M1, p4, M1, p1. (*8 sts*)
Row 4: K1, M1, k6, M1, k1. (*10 sts*)
Starting with a p row, work 7 rows in st st.
Row 12: K1, ssk, k4, k2tog, k1. (*8 sts*)
Row 13: P1, p2tog, p2, p2togtbl, p1. (*6 sts*)
Row 14: K1, ssk, k2tog, k1. (*4 sts*)
Row 15: P2tog, p2togtbl. (*2 sts*)
Thread yarn through rem sts to fasten off.

Tail side 1
*Start at fin section.
Using MC, cast on 2 sts.
Row 1 (WS): Purl.
Row 2: [Kfb] twice. (*4 sts*)
Row 3: P1, M1, p2, M1, p1. (*6 sts*)
Row 4: K1, M1, k4, M1, k1. (*8 sts*)
Row 5: P1, M1, p6, M1, p1. (*10 sts*)
Starting with a k row, work 7 rows in st st.
Row 13: P1, p2tog, p4, p2togtbl, p1. (*8 sts*)
Row 14: K1, ssk, k2, k2tog, k1. (*6 sts*)
Row 15: P1, p2tog, p2togtbl, p1. (*4 sts*)*
Row 16: K1, M1, k to end. (*5 sts*)
Row 17: Purl.
Row 18: K1, M1, k to end. (*6 sts*)
Row 19: P to last st, M1, p1. (*7 sts*)

Row 20: K1, M1, k to end. (*8 sts*)
Place sts on a spare needle.

Tail side 2
Work as for side 1 from * to *.
Row 16: K to last st, M1, k1. (*5 sts*)
Row 17: Purl.
Row 18: K to last st, M1, k1. (*6 sts*)
Row 19: P1, M1, k to end. (*7 sts*)
Row 20: K to last st, M1, k1. (*8 sts*)
Place sts on a spare needle.

Body
Using MC, cast on 8 sts.
Row 1 (WS): Purl.
Row 2: K1, [M1, k2] 3 times, M1, k1. (*12 sts*)
Row 3: Purl.
Row 4: K1, M1, k4, M1, k2, M1, k4, M1, k1. (*16 sts*)
Row 5: P1, M1, p6, M1, p2, M1, p6, M1, p1. (*20 sts*)
Row 6: K1, M1, k8, M1, k2, M1, k8, M1, k1. (*24 sts*)
Row 7: Purl.
Row 8: K1, M1, k10, M1, k2, M1, k10, M1, k1. (*28 sts*)
Row 9: P1, M1, p12, M1, p2, M1, p12, M1, p1. (*32 sts*)
Row 10: K1, M1, k14, M1, k2, M1, k14, M1, k1. (*36 sts*)
Row 11: Purl.
Row 12: K1, M1, k16, M1, k2, M1, k16, M1, k1. (*40 sts*)
Row 13: Purl.
Row 14: K1, M1, k18, M1, k2, M1, k18, M1, k1. (*44 sts*)
Row 15: Purl.
Row 16: K1, M1, k20, M1, k2, M1, k20, M1, k1. (*48 sts*)

90   **oceans, rivers, and lakes**

Row 17: Purl.
Join in CC and another ball of MC and work in intarsia (see page 141).
Row 18: Using MC, k1, M1, k21, using CC, k4, using MC, k21, M1, k1. (*50 sts*)
Row 19: Using MC, p21, using CC, p8, using MC, p21.
Row 20: Using MC, k1, M1, k18, using CC, k4, M1, k4, M1, k4, using MC, k18, M1, k1. (*54 sts*)
Row 21: Using MC, p19, using CC, p16, using MC, p19.
Row 22: Using MC, k1, M1, k17, using CC, k18, using MC, k17, M1, k1. (*56 sts*)
Row 23: Using MC, p18, using CC, p20, using MC, p18.
Row 24: Using MC, k1, M1, k16, using CC, k22, using MC, k16, M1, k1. (*58 sts*)
Row 25: Using MC, p17, using CC, p24, using MC, p17.
Row 26: Using MC, k1, M1, k15, using CC, k26, using MC, k15, M1, k1. (*60 sts*)
Row 27: Using MC, p16, using CC, p28, using MC, p16.
Row 28: Using MC, k1, M1, k14, using CC, k30, using MC, k14, M1, k1. (*62 sts*)
Row 29: Using MC, p14, using CC, p34, using MC, p14.
Row 30: Using MC, k across 8 tail side sts starting at straight edge (not shaped edge), k12, using CC, k38, using MC, k12, k across 8 tail side sts starting at shaped edge (not straight edge). (*78 sts*)
Row 31: Using MC, p18, using CC, p42, using MC, p18.
Row 32: Using MC, k16, using CC, k46, using MC, k16.
Row 33: Using MC, p14, using CC, p50, using MC, p14.
Row 34: Using MC, k12, using CC, k54, using MC, k12.
Row 35: Using MC, p10, using CC, p58, using MC, p10.
Row 36: Using MC, k7, using CC, k64, using MC, k7.
Row 37: Using MC, p4, using CC, p70, using MC, p4.
Break off MC, cont using CC.
Starting with a k row, work 2 rows in st st.
Row 38: K2, ssk, k32, ssk, k2, k2tog, k32, k2tog, k2. (*74 sts*)
Row 39: Purl.
Row 40: K2, ssk, k30, ssk, k2, k2tog, k30, k2tog, k2. (*70 sts*)
Row 41: P2, p2tog, p28, p2tog, p2, p2togtbl, p28, p2togtbl, p2. (*66 sts*)
Row 42: K2, ssk, k26, ssk, k2, k2tog, k26, k2tog, k2. (*62 sts*)
Row 43: P2, p2tog, p22, bind (cast) off 10 sts, p to last 4 sts, p2togtbl, p2. (*2 groups of 25 sts*)
Work on last set of 25 sts only.
Shaping is done with short rows (see page 140).
Row 44: Knit.
Row 45: Purl.
Row 46: K17, turn.
Row 47: Slds, p to end.
Row 48: K11, turn.
Row 49: Slds, p to end.

Row 50: K6, turn.
Row 51: Slds, p to end.
Row 52: Knit.
Leave rem sts on a spare needle.
With RS facing, join yarn to rem 25 sts.
Row 44: Purl.
Row 45: K17, turn.
Row 46: Slds, p to end.
Row 47: K11, turn.
Row 48: Slds, p to end.
Row 49: K6, turn.
Row 50: Slds, p to end.
Row 51: Knit.
Place both sides with RS tog, using third needle, bind (cast) off using three-needle bind (cast) off technique (see page 139).

Making up
Using matching yarn, pin the seam on the body together at the bottom of the front of the head. Sew the seam closed. Pin the cast-on edge at the top of the head together, leaving a length of yarn to sew the rest of the body up. Push the safety eyes through the knitting using the photos as a guide for position. When you are happy with their placement, firmly push the back onto the post of each eye. Continue sewing the seam along the back of the body, adding toy filling as you go. Sew up to the fins.

With the two top fin pieces RS together, sew across the cast-on edges to join them. Pin the top fin pieces to the tail fin sections and sew around each fin.

Using A, embroider the mouth using straight stitch (see page 142). Go back over these stitches, couching the yarn with tiny stitches to make a nice straight mouth.

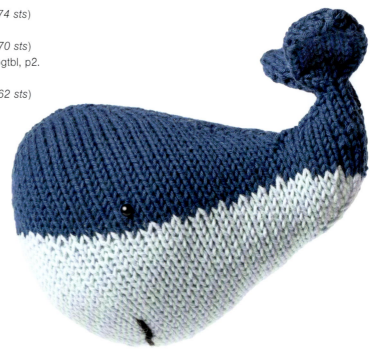

oceans, rivers, and lakes

pudding the hippo

This chunky hippo has nostrils made of little bobbles that are worked as you knit the head. She also has eyebrows, giving her an inquisitive look. Did you know that hippos walk in the water and don't swim?

Skill Level ★★★

Yarn and materials

Rowan Felted Tweed (50% wool, 25% viscose, 25% alpaca) light worsted (DK) weight yarn, 191yd (175m) per 1¾oz (50g) ball

  1 ball of Rose Quartz 206 (light brown)

Small amount of black fingering (4-ply) weight yarn (A)

Pair of 5mm black domed safety eyes

Toy filling

Needles and equipment

US 2 or 3 (3mm) knitting needles

Pair of US 2 or 3 (3mm) double-pointed knitting needles (DPNs)

Yarn needle

Scissors

Pins

Finished size

Foot to top of head excluding ears: 6¾in (17cm)

Nose to rear excluding tail: 6¼in (16cm)

Gauge (tension)

Approx 26 sts to 4in (10cm) measured over stockinette (stocking) stitch using US 2 or 3 (3mm) knitting needles.

Abbreviations

See page 143.

Head

Start at front.
Cast on 16 sts.
Row 1 (WS): Purl.
Row 2: K4, M1, k8, M1, k4. (*18 sts*)
Row 3: Purl.
Row 4: K4, M1, k1, M1, k8, M1, k1, M1, k4. (*22 sts*)
Row 5: Purl.
Row 6: K4, M1, k3, M1, k8, M1, k3, M1, k4. (*26 sts*)
Row 7: Purl.
Row 8: K4, M1, k5, M1, k8, M1, k5, M1, k4. (*30 sts*)
Row 9: Purl.
Row 10: K4, M1, k7, M1, k8, M1, k7, M1, k4. (*34 sts*)
Row 11: Purl.
Row 12: K4, M1, k9, M1, k8, M1, k9, M1, k4. (*38 sts*)
Row 13: Purl.
Row 14: K4, M1, k11, M1, k8, M1, k11, M1, k4. (*42 sts*)
Row 15: Purl.
Row 16: K4, M1, k13, M1, k8, M1, k13, M1, k4. (*46 sts*)
Starting with a p row, work 5 rows in st st.
Row 22: K4, ssk, k11, k2tog, k8, ssk, k11, k2tog, k4. (*42 sts*)
Row 23: Purl.
Row 24: K4, ssk, k9, k2tog, k8, ssk, k9, k2tog, k4. (*38 sts*)
Row 25: P4, p2tog, p7, p2togtbl, p8, p2tog, p7, p2togtbl, p4. (*34 sts*)
Row 26: K11, ssk, k8, k2tog, k11. (*32 sts*)
Row 27: P10, p2tog, p8, p2togtbl, p10. (*30 sts*)
Row 28: K12, M1, k6, M1, k12. (*32 sts*)
Row 29: P13, M1, p6, M1, p13. (*34 sts*)
Row 30: K14, M1, k6, M1, k14. (*36 sts*)
Starting with a p row, work 7 rows in st st.
Row 38: K4, ssk, k7, k2tog, k6, ssk, k7, k2tog, k4. (*32 sts*)
Row 39: Purl.
Row 40: K4, ssk, k5, k2tog, k6, ssk, k5, k2tog, k4. (*28 sts*)
Row 41: Purl.
Row 42: K3, ssk, k5, k2tog, k4, ssk, k5, k2tog, k3. (*24 sts*)
Row 43: P2, p2tog, p5, p2togtbl, p4, p2tog, p5, p2togtbl, p2. (*20 sts*)
Bind (cast) off.

Body

Starting at front of body, worked in two halves.
Cast on 16 sts.
Row 1 (WS): Purl.
Row 2: K2, M1, k to end. (*17 sts*)
Row 3: Purl.
Rep last 2 rows three more times. (*20 sts*)
Starting with a k row, work 4 rows in st st.
Row 14: K to last 2 sts, M1, k2. (*21 sts*)
Row 15: Purl.
Rep last 2 rows once more. (*22 sts*)
Row 18: K to last 2 sts, M1, k2. (*23 sts*)
Break yarn and place sts on spare needle.
SECOND SIDE
With RS facing, pick up and k 16 sts from cast-on edge, purl one row.
NB: This makes a neat join but if you prefer, you can cast on 16 sts instead, foll instructions below from Row 1 and sew seam afterward.

94   **oceans, rivers, and lakes**

Row 1: K to last 2 sts, M1, k2. (*17 sts*)
Row 2: Purl.
Rep last 2 rows three more times. (*20 sts*)
Starting with a k row, work 4 rows in st st.
Row 13: K2, M1, k to end. (*21 sts*)
Row 14: Purl.
Rep last two rows once more. (*22 sts*)
Row 17: K2, M1, k to end. (*23 sts*)
Front shaping creates a space for head to sit. Join front sections as foll:
Row 1: P23, cast on 2 sts, p23 held sts. (*48 sts*)
Starting with a k row, work 24 rows in st st.
Row 26: K2, ssk, k14, ssk, k4, k2tog, k16, k2tog, k2. (*44 sts*)
Row 27: Purl.
Row 28: K2, ssk, k14, ssk, k4, k2tog, k14, k2tog, k2. (*40 sts*)
Row 29: Purl.
Row 30: K2, ssk, k12, ssk, k4, k2tog, k12, k2tog, k2. (*36 sts*)
Row 31: P2, p2tog, p11, p2tog, p2, p2togtbl, p11, p2togtbl, p2. (*32 sts*)
Row 32: K2, ssk, k9, ssk, k2, k2tog, k9, k2tog, k2. (*28 sts*)
Divide rem sts evenly between two needles and, with RS tog and using third needle, bind (cast) off using three-needle bind (cast) off technique (see page 139).

Leg

(make 4)
Cast on 14 sts.
Starting with a k row, work 12 rows in st st.
Shaping is done with short rows (see page 140).
Row 13: K10, turn,
Row 14: Slds, p5, turn.
Row 15: Slds, k4, turn.
Row 16: Slds, p3, turn.
Row 17: Slds, k to end.
Row 18: Purl.
Row 19: Bind (cast) off 5 sts, k to end. (*9 sts*)
Row 20: Bind (cast) off 5 sts, p to end. (*4 sts*)
Row 21: K1, M1, k2, M1, k1. (*6 sts*)
Starting with a p row, work 3 rows in st st.
Row 25: K1, ssk, k2tog, k1. (*4 sts*)
Row 26: P2tog, p2togtbl. (*2 sts*)
Bind (cast) off.

Ear

(make two)
Cast on 3 sts.
Row 1 (WS): Purl.
Row 2: [K1, M1] twice, k1. (*5 sts*)
Row 3: Purl.
Shaping is done with short rows.
Row 4: K4, turn.
Row 5: Slds, p2, turn.
Row 6: Slds, k to end.
Row 7: Purl.
Row 8: Ssk, k1, k2tog. (*3 sts*)
Row 9: CDD. (*1 st*)
Thread yarn through rem st to fasten off.

Nostril

(make two)
Cast on 1 st.
Row 1: Kfb. (*2 sts*)
Row 2: Purl.
Row 3: K2tog.
Thread yarn through rem st to fasten off.

Eyebrow

(make two)
Cast on 7 sts.
Shaping is done with short rows.
Row 1: K6, turn.
Row 2: Slds, p4, turn.
Row 3: Slds, k to end.
Row 4: Purl.
Bind (cast) off, leaving length of yarn for sewing up.

Tail

Using DPNs, cast on 4 sts.
Row 1: K3, push sts to other end of needle, pulling yarn firmly across back of work, without turning.
Rep Row 1 until tail measures 1½in (4cm).
Now work flat.
Starting with a k row, work 2 rows in st st.
Bind (cast) off.

Making up

Stuff the head with toy filling and pin the seam underneath the head together. Using the photos as a guide for position, push the safety eyes through the knitting. With the bound- (cast-) off edge of an eyebrow close to the eye, pin in place so that it curls around the eye. Sew the bound- (cast-) off edge in place and then the cast-on edge, using the photos for guidance as you go. Repeat for second eyebrow. Remove as much toy filling as you can and firmly push the back onto the post of each eye. Re-stuff the head and sew the seams closed. Using the photos for guidance, pin the ears and nostrils to the head. Sew in place. Stuff the body and sew the seam closed. Pin the head to the body and sew firmly in place.

Sew the seam on a leg, placing toy filling in the foot, but not the leg. Repeat for the other three legs. Sew the legs in place on the body with the seams facing toward the back of the hippo.

Using A, make a long curved stitch for the mouth, then take a couple of small catch stitches over it at intervals to hold the curve in place.

TIP It is a good idea to stuff the head and then thread the eyes through the knitting without securing them in place, as once you put the backs on they cannot be moved. Pin on the eyebrows and ears to make sure you get everything in the right place in relation to the eyes, then you can secure the eyes and sew the other features in place.

pudding the hippo 95

Skill Level ★ ★ ★

ribbet the frog

This happy little frog has prominent eyes that are knitted separately and sewn on. At the end of his dangly arms and legs he has three toes, which may seem fiddly but are worth the effort because they give a lovely result.

Yarn and materials
Rowan Felted Tweed (50% wool, 25% viscose, 25% alpaca) light worsted (DK) weight yarn, 191yd (175m) per 1¾oz (50g) ball
    1 ball of Avocado 161 (green)
Small amount of black fingering (4-ply) yarn (or embroidery floss/thread) (A)
Toy filling
Pair of 5mm black domed safety eyes

Needles and equipment
US 2 or 3 (3mm) knitting needles
Spare US 2 or 3 (3mm) knitting needle
Yarn needle
Pins

Finished size
Base to top of head excluding ears:
5½in (14cm)

Gauge (tension)
Approx 26 sts to 10cm (4in) measured over stockinette (stocking) stitch using US 2 or 3 (3mm) knitting needles.

Abbreviations
See page 143.

Body and head
Start at the base.
Cast on 14 sts.
Row 1 (WS): Purl.
Row 2: K2, M1, k to last 2 sts, M1, k2. (*16 sts*)
Row 3: Purl.
Rep last 2 rows twice more. (*20 sts*)
Row 8: K2, ssk, k to last 4 sts, k2tog, k2. (*18 sts*)
Row 9: Purl.
Rep last 2 rows three more times. (*12 sts*)
Row 16: Cast on 16 sts, k to end. (*28 sts*)
Row 17: Cast on 16 sts, p to end. (*44 sts*)
Row 18: K19, M1, k6, M1, k19. (*46 sts*)
Row 19: Purl.
Row 20: K20, M1, k6, M1, k20. (*48 sts*)
Row 21: Purl.
Row 22: K21, M1, k6, M1, k21. (*50 sts*)
Starting with a p row, work 7 rows in st st.
Row 30: K20, ssk, k6, k2tog, k20. (*48 sts*)
Starting with a p row, work 3 rows in st st.
Row 34: K10, ssk, k1, k2tog, k4, ssk, k6, k2tog, k4, ssk, k1, k2tog, k10. (*42 sts*)
Row 35: Purl.
Row 36: K9, ssk, k1, k2tog, k3, ssk, k4, k2tog, k3, ssk, k1, k2tog, k9. (*36 sts*)
Row 37: Purl.
Row 38: K8, ssk, k1, k2tog, k2, ssk, k2, k2tog, k2, ssk, k1, k2tog, k8. (*30 sts*)
Row 39: Purl.
Row 40: Knit.
Row 41: P10, bind (cast) off 10 sts, then p9.
This row forms neck.

Row 42: K10, pick up and k 10 sts from bound- (cast-) off sts, k10. (*30 sts*)
Row 43: Purl.
Row 44: K7, M1, k1, M1, k5, M1, k4, M1, k5, M1, k1, M1, k7. (*36 sts*)
Row 45: Purl.
Row 46: K16, M1, k4, M1, k16. (*38 sts*)
Row 47: Purl.
Row 48: K9, M1, k1, M1, k7, M1, k4, M1, k7, M1, k1, M1, k9. (*44 sts*)
Row 49: Purl.
Shaping is done with short rows (see page 140).
Row 50: K10, M1, k1, M1, k18, turn.
Row 51: Slds, p13, turn.
Row 52: Slds, k11, turn.
Row 53: Slds, p9, turn.
Row 54: Slds, k7, turn.
Row 55: Slds, p5, turn.
Row 56: Slds, k13, M1, k1, M1, k10. (*48 sts*)
Starting with a p row, work 3 rows in st st.
Row 60: K20, ssk, k4, k2tog, k20. (*46 sts*)
Row 61: Purl.
Row 62: K19, ssk, k4, k2tog, k19. (*44 sts*)
Row 63: Purl.
Row 64: K9, ssk, k1, k2tog, k16, ssk, k1, k2tog, k9. (*40 sts*)
Row 65: Purl.
Row 66: K8, ssk, k1, k2tog, k14, ssk, k1, k2tog, k8. (*36 sts*)
Row 67: Purl.
Bind (cast) off.

96 **oceans, rivers, and lakes**

Left arm and hand

Cast on 10 sts.
Starting with a k row, work 28 rows in st st.
*Row 29: K1, M1, k1, turn.
Row 30: P3, turn.
Row 31: K1, kfb, k1. (*4 sts*)
Thread yarn through rem sts to fasten off.
Rejoin yarn to next st on needle.*
Rep from * to * twice more to make three fingers.
Rejoin yarn to next st and bind (cast) off rem 4 sts.

Right arm and hand

Cast on 10 sts.
Starting with a k row, work 28 rows in st st.
Row 29: Bind (cast) off 4 sts, noting st left after bind (cast) off is already worked, *k1, M1, k1, turn.
Row 30: P3, turn.
Row 31: K1, kfb, k1. (*4 sts*)
Thread yarn through rem sts to fasten off.**
Rejoin yarn to next st on needle.*
Rep from * to * once more then from * to ** to make three fingers.

Left leg and foot

*Cast on 10 sts.
Starting with a k row, work 14 rows in st st.
Shaping is done with short rows.
Row 15: K8, turn.
Row 16: Slds, p5, turn.
Row 17: Slds, k4, turn.
Row 18: Slds, p3, turn.
Row 19: Slds, k to end.
Starting with a p row, work 9 rows in st st.*
**Row 29: K1, M1, k1, turn.
Row 30: P3, turn.
Row 31: K1, kfb, k1. (*4 sts*)
Thread yarn through rem sts to fasten off.***
Rejoin yarn to next st on needle.**
Rep from ** to ** once more then from ** to *** to make three toes. Rejoin yarn to next st, bind (cast) off rem 4 sts.

Right leg and foot

Work from * to * as for left leg and foot.
Row 29: Bind (cast) off 4 sts, noting st left after bind (cast) off is already worked, **k1, M1, k1, turn.
Row 30: P3, turn.
Row 31: K1, kfb, k1. (*4 sts*)
Thread yarn through rem sts to fasten off.***
Rejoin yarn to next st on needle.**
Rep from ** to ** once more then from ** to *** to make three toes.

Eye

(make two)
Cast on 14 sts.
Starting with a k row, work 4 rows in st st.
Shaping is done with short rows.
Row 5: K10, turn.
Row 6: Slds, p5, turn.
Row 7: Slds, k to end.
Row 8: Purl.
Row 9: [K1, k2tog] 4 times, k2tog. (*9 sts*)
Row 10: [P2tog] 4 times, p1. (*5 sts*)
Thread yarn through rem sts to fasten off.

Making up

Using matching yarn, sew the seam along the back of the body. Fold the seam at the top of the head as shown in the photos to form a T shape and sew closed. Stuff the body and head with toy filling and then sew the base in place.

Gather the eye and close the bound- (cast-) off stitches, then sew the seam at the back of the eye. Add the safety eyes to knitted eyes by pushing through the knitting, then firmly push the backs onto the post of each eye. Stuff with toy filling. Pin each eye to the top of the head and, when you are happy with their placement, sew in place.

Sew the seam on the inside of each arm. Sew the seam on the hand closed, catching the fingers in place. Repeat for second arm. Pin the arms in place and sew firmly to the body.

Sew the legs together in the same way as the arms and pin to the bottom of the body, using the photos as a guide for position. Sew in place.

Using A, embroider the mouth using backstitch (see page 142).

smiler the axolotl

The axolotl's back fin has a slipped stitch edging and is sewn onto the body in a wavy line.

Skill Level ★★★

Yarn and materials
Rico Ricorumi Spray DK (100% cotton) light worsted (DK) weight yarn, 62yd (57.5m) per ⅞oz (25g) ball
  2¼ balls of Pink 002 (MC)
Small amount of black fingering (4-ply) weight yarn (A)
Toy filling
Pair of 5mm black domed safety eyes

Needles and equipment
US 2 or 3 (3mm) knitting needles
Spare knitting needle for three-needle bind (cast) off
Yarn needle
Scissors
Pins

Finished size
Nose to tip of tail 10⅝in (27cm)

Gauge (tension)
Approx 26 sts to 4in (10cm) measured over stockinette (stocking) stitch using US 2 or 3 (3mm) knitting needles.

Abbreviations
See page 143.

Body and head
Start at end of tail.
Using MC, cast on 5 sts.
Starting with a p row, work 3 rows in st st.
Row 4: K2, M1, k1, M1, k2. (*7 sts*)
Row 5: Purl.
Row 6: K3, M1, k1, M1, k3. (*9 sts*)
Row 7: Purl.
Row 8: K4, M1, k1, M1, k4. (*11 sts*)
Starting with a p row, work 3 rows in st st.
Row 12: K5, M1, k1, M1, k5. (*13 sts*)
Starting with a p row, work 3 rows in st st.
Row 16: K6, M1, k1, M1, k6. (*15 sts*)
Starting with a p row, work 3 rows in st st.
Row 20: K7, M1, k1, M1, k7. (*17 sts*)
Starting with a p row, work 3 rows in st st.
Row 24: K8, M1, k1, M1, k8. (*19 sts*)
Starting with a p row, work 3 rows in st st.
Row 28: K9, M1, k1, M1, k9. (*21 sts*)
Starting with a p row, work 3 rows in st st.
Row 32: K10, M1, k1, M1, k10. (*23 sts*)
Starting with a p row, work 3 rows in st st.
Row 36: K2, M1, k9, M1, k1, M1, k9, M1, k2. (*27 sts*)
Row 37: Purl.
Row 38: K2, M1, k11, M1, k1, M1, k11, M1, k2. (*31 sts*)
Row 39: Purl.
Row 40: K2, M1, k6, M1, k7, M1, k1, M1, k7, M1, k6, M1, k2. (*37 sts*)
Row 41: Purl.
Row 42: K2, M1, k8, M1, k8, M1, k1, M1, k8, M1, k8, M1, k2. (*43 sts*)
Starting with a p row, work 21 rows in st st.
Row 64: K2, ssk, k7, ssk, k6, ssk, k1, k2tog, k6, k2tog, k7, k2tog, k2. (*37 sts*)
Starting with a p row, work 3 rows in st st.

Row 68: K2, ssk, k5, ssk, k5, ssk, k1, k2tog, k5, k2tog, k5, k2tog, k2. (*31 sts*)
Row 69: Purl.
Row 70: K2, ssk, k3, ssk, k4, ssk, k1, k2tog, k4, k2tog, k3, k2tog, k2. (*25 sts*)
Row 71: Purl.
Row 72: K2, M1, k4, M1, k2, M1, k4, M1, k1, M1, k4, M1, k2, M1, k4, M1, k2. (*33 sts*)
Row 73: Purl.
Row 74: K2, M1, k6, M1, k2, M1, k6, M1, k1, M1, k6, M1, k2, M1, k6, M1, k2. (*41 sts*)
Row 75: Purl.
Row 76: K10, M1, k21, M1, k10. (*43 sts*)
Starting with a p row, work 9 rows in st st.
Row 86: K8, ssk, k1, k2tog, k17, ssk, k1, k2tog, k8. (*39 sts*)
Row 87: Purl.
Row 88: K7, ssk, k1, k2tog, k3, ssk, k5, k2tog, k3, ssk, k1, k2tog, k7. (*33 sts*)
Row 89: P6, p2tog, p1, p2togtbl, p1, p2tog, p5, p2togtbl, p1, p2tog, p1, p2togtbl, p6. (*27 sts*)
Row 90: K5, ssk, k1, k2tog, k7, ssk, k1, k2tog, k5. (*23 sts*)
Row 91: P4, p2tog, p1, p2togtbl, p5, p2tog, p1, p2togtbl, p4. (*19 sts*)
Bind (cast) off.

Top spine
Using MC, cast on 3 sts.
Slip sts purlwise to avoid them twisting.
Row 1: K1, sl2 wyif.
Row 2: Knit.
Row 3: Kfb, sl2 wyif. (*4 sts*)
Row 4: Knit.
Row 5: K2, sl2 wyif.
Row 6: Knit.
Row 7: K1, kfb, sl2 wyif. (*5 sts*)
Row 8: Knit.

100 oceans, rivers, and lakes

Row 9: K3, sl2 wyif.
Row 10: Knit.*
Row 11: K2, kfb, sl2 wyif. (*6 sts*)
Row 12: Knit.
Row 13: K4, sl2 wyif.
Row 14: Knit.
Row 15: K3, kfb, sl2 wyif. (*7 sts*)
Row 16: Knit.
Row 17: K5, sl2 wyif.
Row 18: Knit.
Rep last 2 rows eight more times.
Row 35: K2tog, k3, sl2 wyif. (*6 sts*)
Row 36: Knit.
Row 37: K2tog, k2, sl2 wyif. (*5 sts*)
Row 38: Knit.
Row 39: K2tog, k1, sl2 wyif. (*4 sts*)
Row 40: Knit.
Row 41: K2tog, sl2 wyif. (*3 sts*)
Row 42: Knit.
Row 43: K2, sl2 wyif.
Row 44: Knit.
Row 45: K2tog, sl1 wyif. (*2 sts*)
Row 46: K2tog. (*1 st*)
Thread yarn through rem st to fasten off.

Bottom spine
Using MC, cast on 3 sts.
Work as for top spine from * to *.
Row 11: K3, sl2 wyif.
Row 12: Knit.
Rep last 2 rows eleven more times.
Row 35: K2tog, k1, sl2 wyif. (*4 sts*)
Row 36: Knit.
Row 37: K2tog, sl2 wyif. (*3 sts*)
Row 38: Knit.
Row 39: K1, sl2 wyif.
Row 40: Knit.
Row 41: K2tog, sl1 wyif. (*2 sts*)
Row 42: K2tog. (*1 st*)
Thread yarn through rem st to fasten off.

Frill pieces
(make six)
Using MC, cast on 5 sts.
Row 4: Bind (cast) off 2 sts, sl1 st back to LH needle, [cast on 4 sts, bind (cast) off 2 sts, sl st back to LH needle] 6 times, cast on 1 st. (*18 sts*)
Divide rem sts evenly between two needles and, with RS tog fold so needles are parallel and using third needle, bind (cast) off using three-needle bind (cast) off technique (see page 139).

Leg
(make four)
Using MC, cast on 4 sts.
Row 1 (WS): Purl.
Row 2: K1, M1, k to last st, M1, k1. (*6 sts*)

Row 3: Purl.
Rep last 2 rows once more. (*8 sts*)
Starting with a k row, work 8 rows in st st.
Row 14: K3, M1, k2, M1, k3. (*10 sts*)
Row 15: Purl.
Row 16: K4, M1, k2, M1, k4. (*12 sts*)
Row 17: Purl.
Row 18: K3, ssk, k2, k2tog, k3. (*10 sts*)
Row 19: P2, p2tog, p2, p2togtbl, p2. (*8 sts*)
Divide rem sts evenly between two needles and, with RS tog and using third needle, bind (cast) off using three-needle bind (cast) off technique.

Making up
Pin the head together and stuff with toy filling. Add the safety eyes to the head by pushing through the knitting using the photos as a guide for position. When you are happy with the placement, remove the pins and toy filling and firmly push the backs onto the post of each eye.

Starting at the tail, sew the seam underneath the body, stuffing with toy filling as you go. Stuff the head again and sew the bound- (cast-) off edges together with the body seam underneath the head.

Pin the top spine in place along the tail, using the photos for guidance. The tail needs to be "wavy," so pin the spine on so that it curves slightly along the body. Sew in place. Then pin the bottom spine under the body, and sew in position.

Gather the bound- (cast-) off edge of the leg and sew the side seam, stuffing the foot with toy filling as you go. Leave the leg unstuffed. Repeat for the other legs. Pin each leg in place, using the photos for guidance, and sew in place.

Pin the frill pieces in place with three on each side of the head, with the bound- (cast-) off edges facing toward the back. Sew in place.

Using A, embroider the mouth using backstitch (see page 142).

Skill Level ★ ★ ★

twinkle the starfish

The top of this cute starfish is knitted in garter stitch with a central decrease
in stockinette (stocking) stitch. On the reverse, each arm has a row of bobbles.

Yarn and materials
Rico Ricorumi Spray DK (100% cotton)
light worsted (DK) weight yarn, 62yd
(57.5m) per ⅞oz (25g) ball
  2¼ balls of Pink 002

Small amount of black fingering (4-ply)
weight yarn (A)

Pair of 5mm black domed safety eyes

Toy filling

Needles and equipment
US 2 or 3 (3mm) knitting needles

Spare knitting needles or stitch holders

Yarn needle

Scissors

Pins

Finished size
Width at widest point: 6in (15cm)

Gauge (tension)
Approx 26 sts to 4in (10cm) measured
over stockinette (stocking) stitch using
US 2 or 3 (3mm) knitting needles.

Abbreviations
See page 143.

Special abbreviation
MB (make bobble): Kfb, turn, p2, turn, k2,
slip second st from end of needle over
first st. *(1 st)*

Top of tentacle
(make 5)
Cast on 7 sts.
Row 1 (WS): K2, p3, k2.
Row 2: Kfb, k1, CDD, k1, kfb.
Row 3: Kfb, k1, p3, k1, kfb. (*9 sts*)
Row 4: Kfb, k2, CDD, k2, kfb.
Row 5: Kfb, k2, p3, k2, kfb. (*11 sts*)
Row 6: Kfb, k3, CDD, k3, kfb.
Row 7: Kfb, k3, p3, k3, kfb. (*13 sts*)
Row 8: Kfb, k4, CDD, k4, kfb.
Row 9: Kfb, k4, p3, k4, kfb. (*15 sts*)
Row 10: Kfb, k5, CDD, k5, kfb.
Row 11: K6, p3, k6.
Place rem sts on spare needle or st holder.

Joining top
Place all five top tentacles on same needle with RS facing
and join as foll:
Row 1: K6, [CDD, k12] 4 times, CDD, k6. (*65 sts*)
Row 2: K5, [p3, k10] 4 times, p3, k5.
Row 3: K5, [CDD, k10] 4 times, CDD, k5. (*55 sts*)
Row 4: K4, [p3, k8] 4 times, p3, k4.
Row 5: K4, [CDD, k8] 4 times, CDD, k4. (*45 sts*)
Row 6: K3, [p3, k6] 4 times, p3, k3.
Row 7: K3, [CDD, k6] 4 times, CDD, k3. (*35 sts*)
Row 8: K2, [p3, k4] 4 times, p3, k2.
Row 9: K2, [CDD, k4] 4 times, CDD, k2. (*25 sts*)
Row 10: K1, [p3, k2] 4 times, p3, k1.
Row 11: K1, [CDD, k2] 4 times, CDD, k1. (*15 sts*)
Row 12: Purl.
Thread yarn through rem sts to fasten off.

Bottom of tentacle
(make 5)
Cast on 3 sts.
Starting with a k row, work 2 rows in st st.
Row 3: K1, M1, MB, M1, k1. (*5 sts*)
Row 4: Purl.
Row 5: Knit.
Row 6: Purl.
Row 7: K1, M1, k1, MB, k1, M1, k1. (*7 sts*)
Row 8: Purl.
Row 9: Knit.
Row 10: Purl.
Row 11: K1, M1, k2, MB, k2, M1, k1. (*9 sts*)
Row 12: Purl.
Row 13: Knit.
Row 14: Purl.
Row 15: K1, M1, k3, MB, k3, M1, k1. (*11 sts*)
Row 16: Purl.
Place rem sts on spare needle or st holder.

Joining bottom
Place all 5 bottom tentacles on same needle with RS facing and
join as foll:
Row 1: K across all sts. (*55 sts*)
Row 2: Purl.
Row 3: K2tog, k3, [MB, k3, ssk, k2tog, k3] 4 times, MB, k3,
ssk. (*45 sts*)
Row 4: Purl.
Row 5: K2tog, [k5, ssk, k2tog] 4 times, k5, ssk. (*35 sts*)
Row 6: Purl.
Row 7: K2tog, [k1, MB, k1, ssk, k2tog] 4 times, k1, MB, k1, ssk.
(*25 sts*)
Row 8: Purl.
Row 9: K2tog, [k1, ssk, k2tog] 4 times, k1, ssk. (*15 sts*)
Row 10: Purl.

102 oceans, rivers, and lakes

Row 11: [K2tog] 7 times, k1. (*8 sts*)
Thread yarn through rem sts to fasten off.

Making up

Sew the side edges of top and bottom from the start of the joining rows to the center. Add the safety eyes to the top of the starfish by pushing through the knitting using the photos as a guide for position. When you are happy with the placement, firmly push the backs onto the post of each eye.

Pin the top to the bottom with WS together, easing to fit. Sew around each tentacle, stuffing as you go. When you reach the last one, check there is enough toy filling in the body then sew the remaining tentacle together.

Using A, embroider the mouth using straight stitches (see page 142).

twinkle the starfish 103

Skill Level ★★★

inky the octopus

The legs of this friendly octopus are knitted separately, then the tops of the legs are joined to make the body.

Yarn and materials
Rico Ricorumi Print DK (100% cotton) light worsted (DK) weight yarn, 62yd (57.5m) per ⅞oz (25g) ball

2¼ balls of Multicolor 004 (MC)

Rico Ricorumi DK (100% cotton) light worsted (DK) weight yarn, 63yd (58m) per ⅞oz (25g) ball

¾ ball of Aqua 074 (turquoise) (CC)

Small amount of black fingering (4-ply) weight yarn (A)

Pair of 5mm black domed safety eyes

Toy filling

Needles and equipment
US 2 or 3 (3mm) knitting needles

Spare knitting needles or stitch holders

Yarn needle

Scissors

Pins

Finished size
Top of head to end of tentacle: 8¾in (22cm)

Gauge (tension)
Approx 26 sts to 4in (10cm) measured over stockinette (stocking) stitch using US 2 or 3 (3mm) knitting needles.

Abbreviations
See page 143.

Special abbreviation
MB (make bobble): Kfb, turn, p2, turn, k2, slip second st from end of needle over first st. (*1 st*)

Top of tentacle
(make eight)
Using MC, cast on 5 sts.
Starting with a k row, work 2 rows in st st.
Row 3: K1, M1, k3, M1, k1. (*7 sts*)
Starting with a p row, work 5 rows in st st.
Row 9: K1, M1, k5, M1, k1. (*9 sts*)

Starting with a p row, work 37 rows in st st.
Row 47: K2, ssk, k1, k2tog, k2. (*7 sts*)
Row 48: Purl.
Break yarn and place sts on spare needle or st holder.

Joining top
Place all 8 top tentacles on one needle, with RS facing.
Row 1: K6, [k2tog, k5] 6 times, k2tog, k6. (*49 sts*)
Row 2: Purl.
Row 3: K2tog, k3, [CDD, k3] 7 times, k2. (*34 sts*)
Row 4: Purl.
Row 5: Knit.
Row 6: Purl.
Row 7: K1, M1, k3, [M1, k1, M1, k3] 7 times, M1, k2. (*50 sts*)
Starting with a p row, work 15 rows in st st.
Row 23: K1, [k2tog, k5] 7 times. (*43 sts*)
Row 24: Purl.
Row 25: K1, [k2tog, k4] 7 times. (*36 sts*)
Row 26: Purl.
Row 27: K1, [k2tog, k3] 7 times. (*29 sts*)
Row 28: Purl.
Row 29: K1, [k2tog, k2] 6 times, k2tog, k2. (*22 sts*)
Row 30: [P2tog] 11 times. (*11 sts*)
Row 31: [K2tog] 5 times, k1. (*6 sts*)
Thread yarn through rem sts to fasten off.

Bottom of tentacle
(make eight)
Using CC, cast on 3 sts.
Starting with a k row, work 2 rows in st st.
Row 3: [K1, M1] twice, k1. (*5 sts*)
Row 4: Purl.
Row 5: K2, MB, k2.
Row 6: Purl.
Row 7: Knit.
Row 8: Purl.
Row 9: K2, MB, k2.
Row 10: Purl.
Row 11: K1, M1, k3, M1, k1. (*7 sts*)
Row 12: Purl.
Row 13: K2, MB, k1, MB, k2.

Row 14: Purl.
Row 15: Knit.
Row 16: Purl.
Rep last 4 rows eight more times.
Break yarn and place sts on spare needle or st holder.

Joining bottom
Place all 8 bottom tentacles on one needle, with RS facing.
Row 1: K6, [k2tog, k5] 6 times, k2tog, k6. (*49 sts*)
Row 2: Purl.
Row 3: K2tog, k3, [CDD, k3] 7 times, k2. (*34 sts*)
Row 4: Purl.
Row 5: K2tog, k1, [CDD, k1] 7 times, k1, k2tog. (*18 sts*)
Row 6: Purl.
Row 7: [K2tog] 9 times. (*9 sts*)
Thread yarn through rem sts to fasten off.

Making up
Pin the seam at the top of the octopus together, which will be at the back of the body. Stuff with toy filling. Add the safety eyes to the head by pushing through the knitting using the photos as a guide for position. When you are happy with the placement, remove the pins and toy filling and firmly push the backs onto the post of each eye.

Starting at the top of the head, sew the seam to the base of the body, stuffing with toy filling as you go.

At the bottom of the octopus, sew the seam from the middle of the body to the edge, where the legs start.

Pin the top tentacles to the bottom tentacles. Starting at the body, sew along one edge of a tentacle, around the end, and along the other side, placing a small amount of toy filling inside to add definition. Repeat this process until all eight tentacles are sewn up.

Using A, and with the photos as a guide, embroider the face using straight stitches.

inky the octopus 105

Skill Level ★ ★ ★

neptune the seahorse

This sweet seahorse is knitted in one piece from the end of its curly tail to the tip of its nose.

Yarn and materials
Rico Ricorumi Spray DK (100% cotton) light worsted (DK) weight yarn, 62yd (57.5m) per 7/8oz (25g) ball
2¼ balls of Pink 002

Toy filling

Pair of 5mm black domed safety eyes

Needles and equipment
US 2 or 3 (3mm) knitting needles

Yarn needle

Scissors

Pins

Finished size
Height: 8¼in (21cm)

Gauge (tension)
Approx 26 sts to 4in (10cm) measured over stockinette (stocking) stitch using US 2 or 3 (3mm) knitting needles.

Abbreviations
See page 143.

Body and head
Start at tail.
Cast on 4 sts.
Row 1 (WS): Purl.
Row 2: K1, M1, k2, M1, k1. (*6 sts*)
Row 3: Purl.
Shaping is done with short rows (see page 140).
***Row 4:** K5, turn.
Row 5: Slds, p3, turn.
Row 6: Slds, k to end.
Row 7: Knit.*
Rep from * to * nine more times.
Row 44: K1, M1, k4, M1, k1. (*8 sts*)
Row 45: Purl.
Row 46: K1, M1, k6, M1, k1. (*10 sts*)
Row 47: P1, M1, p8, M1, p1. (*12 sts*)
Row 48: K1, M1, k2, p2, M1, p2, M1, p2, k2, M1, k1. (*16 sts*)
Row 49: Purl.
Row 50: K1, M1, k6, M1, k2, M1, k6, M1, k1. (*20 sts*)

Row 51: P1, M1, p to last st, M1, p1. (*22 sts*)
Row 52: K1, M1, k4, p5, M1, p2, M1, p5, k4, M1, k1. (*26 sts*)
Row 53: P1, M1, p to last st, M1, p1. (*28 sts*)
Row 54: K1, M1, k12, M1, k2, M1, k12, M1, k1. (*32 sts*)
Row 55: P1, M1, p to last st, M1, p1. (*34 sts*)
Row 56: K1, M1, k6, p20, k6, M1, k1. (*36 sts*)
Row 57: Purl.
Row 58: K1, M1, k to last st, M1, k1. (*38 sts*)
Row 59: Purl.
Row 60: K8, p22, k8.
Row 61: Purl.
Row 62: Knit.
Row 63: Purl.
Rep last 4 rows twice more.
Row 72: K2, ssk, k to last 4 sts, k2tog, k2. (*36 sts*)
Row 73: Purl.
Row 74: K2, ssk, k3, p20, k3, k2tog, k2. (*34 sts*)
Row 75: Purl.
Row 76: K2, ssk, k3, p20, k2tog, k2. (*32 sts*)
Row 77: P2, p2tog, p to last 4 sts, p2togtbl, p2. (*30 sts*)
Row 78: K2, ssk, k to last 4 sts, k2tog, k2. (*28 sts*)
Row 79: P2, p2tog, p to last 4 sts, p2togtbl, p2. (*26 sts*)
Row 80: K2, ssk, k1, p16, k1, k2tog, k2. (*24 sts*)
Row 81: P2, p2tog, p to last 4 sts, p2togtbl, p2. (*22 sts*)
Row 82: K19, turn.
Row 83: Slds, p15, turn.
Row 84: Slds, k12, turn.
Row 85: Slds, p9, turn.
Row 86: Slds, k6, turn.
Row 87: Slds, p3, turn.
Row 88: Slds, k to end.
Row 89: Purl.
Row 90: K4, p14, k1, turn.
Row 91: Slds, p15, turn.

Row 92: Slds, k12, turn.
Row 93: Slds, p9, turn.
Row 94: Slds, k6, turn.
Row 95: Slds, p3, turn.
Row 96: Slds, k to end.
Row 97: Purl.
Rep Rows 90–97 once more.
Row 106: K19.
Row 107: Slds.
Row 108: Slds.
Row 109: Slds.
Row 110: Slds.
Row 111: Slds.
Row 112: Slds.
Row 113: Purl.
Row 114: [K2, k2tog] 5 times, k2. (*17 sts*)
Row 115: Purl.
Row 116: [K2tog] 8 times, k1. (*9 sts*)
Row 117: Purl.
Row 118: K1, ssk, k3, k2tog, k1. (*7 sts*)
Starting with a k row, work 5 rows in st st.
Row 124: Purl (forms ridge).
Row 125: [K2tog] 3 times, k1. (*4 sts*)
Thread yarn through rem sts to fasten off.

Wing
(make two)
Cast on 9 sts.
Row 1: [K1tbl, p1] 4 times, k1tbl.
Row 2: [P1, k1tbl] 4 times, p1.
Row 3: [K1tbl, p1] 4 times, k1tbl.
Row 4: [P1, k1tbl] 4 times, p1.
Row 5: K1tbl, M1, [p1, k1tbl] 3 times, p1, M1, k1tbl. (*11 sts*)
Row 6: Bind (cast) off 3 sts, then [k1tbl, p1] 3 times, k1tbl. (*8 sts*)
Row 7: Bind (cast) off 3 sts, then [p1, k1tbl] twice. (*5 sts*)
Bind (cast) off rem 5 sts.

Spine
Cast on 40 sts.
Row 1: Knit.
Row 2: Bind (cast) off 2 sts, then *sl st from LH needle to RH needle, cast on 2 sts, bind (cast) off 4 sts.*
Work from * to * until 1 st rem, bind (cast) off.

106   oceans, rivers, and lakes

Making up

Pin the head together and stuff with toy filling. Add the safety eyes to the head by pushing through the knitting using the photos as a guide for position. When you are happy with the placement, remove the pins and toy filling and firmly push the backs onto the post of each eye.

Starting at the tip of the tail, sew the seam pulling the yarn as you go—this will encourage the tail to curl round. Continue sewing the seam, stuffing with toy filling as you go. When you reach the neck make sure there is enough toy filling in the neck to make the head curl over. Continue sewing the seam, gathering the bound- (cast-) off edge together, stuffing the head as you go.

Pin the spine in place down the back. When you are happy with the placement, sew in place.

Pin a wing on each side of the body with the bound- (cast-) off edge toward the back and making sure they are level. Sew the wings to the body.

Skill Level ★★★

coco the clownfish

This cheeky little fish includes some colorwork and short-row shaping which together create the colored blocks on the body.

Yarn and materials
Rico Ricorumi DK (100% cotton) light worsted (DK) weight yarn, 63yd (58m) per ⅞oz (25g) ball
  ¾ ball of Black 060 (MC)
  1 ball of Orange 027 (CC1)
  1 ball of White 001 (CC2)

Small amount of black fingering (4-ply) weight yarn (A)

Toy filling

Pair of 5mm black domed safety eyes

Needles and equipment
US 2 or 3 (3mm) knitting needles

Spare knitting needle for three-needle bind (cast) off

2 stitch holders

Yarn needle

Scissors

Pins

Finished size
Length: 7¾in (20cm)

Gauge (tension)
Approx 26 sts to 4in (10cm) measured over stockinette (stocking) stitch using US 2 or 3 (3mm) knitting needles.

Abbreviations
See page 143.

Body and head side 1
Start at tail.
Using MC, cast on 3 sts, bind (cast) off 1 st, slip st from RH needle back onto LH needle, [cast on 2 sts, bind (cast) off 1 st, slip st from RH needle back onto LH needle] 10 times. (*12 sts*)
Row 1 (WS): Purl.
Change to CC1.
Row 2: Knit.
Shaping is done with short rows (see page 140).
*Row 3: P8, turn.
Row 4: Slds, k3, turn.

Row 5: Slds, p4, turn.
Row 6: Slds, k5, turn.
Row 7: Slds, p6, turn.
Row 8: Slds, k7, turn.
Row 9: Slds, p8, turn.
Row 10: Slds, k to end.
Row 11: Purl.
Row 12: K1, ssk, k6, k2tog, k1. (*10 sts*)
Change to MC.
Row 13: Purl.
Change to CC2.
Row 14: Knit.
Row 15: P4, turn.
Row 16: Slds, k to end.
Row 17: P1, p2tog, p to end. (*9 sts*)
Row 18: K4, turn.
Row 19: Slds, p2togtbl, p1. (*8 sts*)
Row 20: Knit.
Row 21: P1, M1, p to last st, M1, p1. (*10 sts*)
Change to MC.
Row 22: K1, M1, k to last st, M1, k1. (*12 sts*)
Change to CC1.
Row 23: Purl.
Row 24: K1, M1, k7, turn. (*13 sts*)
Row 25: Slds, p4, turn.
Row 26: Slds, k to last st, M1, k1. (*14 sts*)
Row 27: Purl.
Row 28: K1, M1, k to last st, M1, k1. (*16 sts*)
Row 29: Purl.
Rep last 2 rows once more. (*18 sts*)
Row 32: K1, M1, k14, turn. (*19 sts*)
Row 33: Slds, p11, turn.
Row 34: Slds, k to last st, M1, k1. (*20 sts*)
Row 35: Purl.
Row 36: K1, M1, k to last st, M1, k1. (*22 sts*)
Row 37: Purl.
Change to MC.
Row 38: Knit.
Change to CC2.
Row 39: Purl.
Row 40: Knit.
Row 41: Purl.
Row 42: K6, turn.

Row 43: Slds, p to end.
Row 44: Knit.
Row 45: P6, turn.
Row 46: Slds, k to end.
Row 47: Purl.
Row 48: K16, turn.
Row 49: Slds, p9, turn.
Row 50: Slds, k6, turn.
Row 51: Slds, p3, turn.
Row 52: Slds, k to end.
Row 53: Purl.
Change to MC.
Row 54: Knit.
Change to CC1.
Row 55: Purl.
Row 56: K9, turn.
Row 57: Slds, p to end.
Row 58: K6, turn.
Row 59: Slds, p to end.
Row 60: Knit.
Row 61: P9, turn.
Row 62: Slds, k to end.
Row 63: P6, turn.
Row 64: Slds, k to end.
Row 65: Purl.
Row 66: K1, ssk, k to last 3 sts, k2tog, k1. (*20 sts*)
Row 67: Purl.
Row 68: K9, turn.
Row 69: Slds, p to end.
Row 70: K1, ssk, k3, turn. (*19 sts*)
Row 71: Slds, p to end.
Row 72: Knit.
Row 73: P9, turn.
Row 74: Slds, k to end.
Row 75: P6, turn.
Row 76: Slds, k2, k2tog, k1. (*18 sts*)
Row 77: Purl.
Change to MC.
Row 78: Knit.
Change to CC2.
Row 79: Purl.
Row 80: K1, ssk, k to last 3 sts, k2tog, k1. (*16 sts*)
Row 81: Purl.
Row 82: K1, ssk, k to last 3 sts, k2tog, k1. (*14 sts*)
Change to MC.
Row 83: Purl.

108 oceans, rivers, and lakes

Change to CC1.
Row 84: Knit.
Row 85: P9, turn.
Row 86: Slds, k3, turn.
Row 87: Slds, p to end.
Row 88: K1, ssk, k to last 3 sts, k2tog, k1. (*12 sts*)
Row 89: Purl.
Rep last 2 rows once more. (*10 sts*)
Row 92: K1, ssk, k to last 3 sts, k2tog, k1. (*8 sts*)
Row 93: P1, p2tog, p2, p2togtbl, p1. (*6 sts*)*
Place rem sts on st holder.

Body and head side 2
Using CC1, cast on 12 sts.
Row 1: Knit.
Work as for side 1 from * to *.
Place 6 rem sts on each side of body on two needles. With RS tog and using third needle, bind (cast) off using three-needle bind (cast) off technique (see page 139).

Fin top and bottom
(make eight)
Using MC, cast on 10 sts. Change to CC1.
Row 1: Knit.
Shaping is done with short rows.
Row 2: P7, turn.
Row 3: Slds, k3, turn.
Row 4: Slds, p4, turn.
Row 5: Slds, k5, turn.
Row 6: Slds, p6, turn.
Row 7: Slds, k7, turn.
Row 8: Slds, p to end.
Bind (cast) off.

Side fin
(make two)
Using MC, cast on 10 sts. Change to CC1.
Row 1 (RS): Knit.
Shaping is done with short rows.
Row 2: P7, turn.
Row 3: Slds, k3, turn.
Row 4: Slds, p4, turn.
Row 5: Slds, k5, turn.
Row 6: Slds, p6, turn.
Row 7: Slds, k7, turn.
Row 8: Slds, p to end.
Row 9: K1, ssk, k4, k2tog, k1. (*8 sts*)
Row 10: P1, p2tog, p2, p2togtbl, p1. (*6 sts*)
Bind (cast) off.

Making up
Pin the head together and stuff with toy filling. Add the safety eyes to the head by pushing through the knitting using the photos as a guide for position. When you are happy with the placement, firmly push the backs onto the post of each eye.

Starting at the top of the head, sew along the top seam, using matching yarn. At the tail, sew the CC1 cast-on edge to the CC1 section immediately underneath the MC end of the tail on the other body piece. Leave the tail unstuffed and start sewing the seam underneath the fish, stuffing the body with toy filling as you go, using matching yarn.

Using MC, sew two top and bottom fin pieces WS together along the top edge. Sew the bottom seam closed using CC1. Repeat for the remaining three fins. Using the photos for guidance, pin the fins in place. When you are happy with their placement, sew firmly in place along each edge.

Pin the side fins in place on each side, making sure they are level. When you are happy with their placement, sew in place.

Using the photo on page 75 as a guide and A, embroider the face using backstitch (see page 142).

TIP Don't worry if the body appears misshapen—once the fish is sewn together and stuffed, it will all even out.

coco the clownfish 109

Chapter 4
skies and trees

shadow the bat

This little bat has garter stitch wings with an applied i-cord, which adds to their structure. The wings fold up and are secured with a little button, so that you can hang your bat upside down by the little loops on the back of the legs.

Skill Level ★★★

Yarn and materials
Rowan Felted Tweed (50% wool, 25% viscose, 25% alpaca) light worsted (DK) weight yarn, 191yd (175m) per 1¾oz (50g) ball
  ½ ball of shade Treacle 145 (MC)
Small amount of black fingering (4-ply) yarn (or embroidery floss/thread) (A)
Toy filling
Pair of 5mm black domed safety eyes
Matching cotton sewing thread
Small button (I used a ¼in/5mm button)

Needles and equipment
US 2 or 3 (3mm) knitting needles
US 2 or 3 (3mm) double-pointed needles (DPNs)
Stitch markers
Yarn needle
Sewing needle
Scissors
Pins

Finished size
Foot to top of head: 4¼in (11cm)
Wing tip to wing tip: 6¼in (16cm)

Gauge (tension)
Approx 26 sts to 4in (10cm) measured over stockinette (stocking) stitch using US 2 or 3 (3mm) knitting needles.

Abbreviations
See page 143.

Body and head
Start at base of body.
Using MC, cast on 22 sts.
Row 1: Purl.
Row 2 (RS): K5, M1, k1, M1, k10, M1, k1, M1, k5. (26 sts)
Row 3: Purl.
Row 4: K6, M1, k1, M1, k12, M1, k1, M1, k6. (30 sts)
Row 5: P7, M1, p1, M1, p14, M1, p1, M1, p7. (34 sts)
Row 6: K8, M1, k1, M1, k16, M1, k1, M1, k8. (38 sts)
Row 7: Purl.
Row 8: K9, M1, k1, M1, k18, M1, k1, M1, k9. (42 sts)
Row 9: Purl.
Shaping is done with short rows (see page 140).
Row 10: K27, turn.
Row 11: Slds, p11, turn.
Row 12: Slds, k12, turn.
Row 13: Slds, p13, turn.
Row 14: Slds, k11, turn.
Row 15: Slds, p9, turn.
Row 16: Slds, k to end.
Starting with a p row, work 5 rows in st st.
Row 22: K8, ssk, k1, k2tog, k16, ssk, k1, k2tog, k8. (38 sts)
Row 23: Purl.
Row 24: K7, ssk, k1, k2tog, k14, ssk, k1, k2tog, k7. (34 sts)
Row 25: Purl.
Row 26: K6, ssk, k1, k2tog, k12, ssk, k1, k2tog, k6. (30 sts)
Row 27: P5, p2tog, p1, p2togtbl, p10, p2tog, p1, p2togtbl, p5. (26 sts)
Row 28: K4, ssk, k1, k2tog, k8, ssk, k1, k2tog, k4. (22 sts)
Row 29: Purl.
Row 30: K3, ssk, k1, k2tog, k6, ssk, k1, k2tog, k3. (18 sts)
Row 31: Purl.

112 skies and trees

Inc for head as foll:
Row 32: K4, M1, k1, M1, k3, M1, k2, M1, k3, M1, k1, M1, k4. (*24 sts*)
Row 33: Purl.
Row 34: K5, M1, k1, M1, k5, M1, k2, M1, k5, M1, k1, M1, k5. (*30 sts*)
Row 35: Purl.
Row 36: P14, M1, k2, M1, p14. (*32 sts*)
Row 37: K19, turn.
Row 38: Slds, p5, turn.
Row 39: Slds, k4, turn.
Row 40: Slds, p3, turn.
Row 41: K to end.
Starting with a p row, work 3 rows in st st.
Row 45: K5, ssk, k1, k2tog, k12, ssk, k1, k2tog, k5. (*28 sts*)
Row 46: Purl.
Row 47: K4, ssk, k1, k2tog, k10, ssk, k1, k2tog, k4. (*24 sts*)
Row 48: Purl.
Row 49: K3, ssk, k1, k2tog, k8, ssk, k1, k2tog, k3. (*20 sts*)
Row 50: P5, p2togtbl, p6, p2tog, p5. (*18 sts*)
Bind (cast) off rem sts, leaving length of yarn for sewing up.

Left foot and leg
Starting at foot.
Using MC, cast on 6 sts.
Row 1 (WS): [P2, M1] twice, p2. (*8 sts*)
Shaping is done with short rows.
Row 2: K6, turn.
Row 3: Slds, p3, turn.
Row 4: Slds, k2, turn.
Row 5: Slds, p to end.
Row 6: Knit.
Row 7: P2, p2tog, p2togtbl, p2. (*6 sts*)
Starting with a k row, work 2 rows in st st.
Row 10: K3, turn.
Row 11: Slds, p to end.
Row 12: Knit.
Bind (cast) off, leaving length of yarn for sewing up.

Right foot and leg
Starting at foot.
Using MC, cast on 6 sts.
Row 1 (RS): [K2, M1] twice, k2. (*8 sts*)
Shaping is done with short rows.
Row 2: P6, turn.
Row 3: Slds, k3, turn.
Row 4: Slds, p2, turn.
Row 5: Slds, k to end.
Row 6: Purl.
Row 7: K2, ssk, k2tog, k2. (*6 sts*)
Starting with a p row, work 2 rows in st st.
Row 10: P3, turn.
Row 11: Slds, k to end.
Row 12: Purl.
Bind (cast) off, leaving length of yarn for sewing up.

114   skies and trees

Wing

(make two)
Using MC, cast on 12 sts.
Row 1: K to last 3 sts, sl3 wyif.
Row 2: Knit.
Rep last 2 rows once more.
Row 5: K to last 4 sts, kfb, sl3 wyif. (*13 sts*)
Row 6: Knit.
Row 7: K to last 4 sts, kfb, sl3 wyif. (*14 sts*)
Row 8: K to last 2 sts, kfb, k1. (*15 sts*)
Rep last 4 rows once more. (*18 sts*)
Row 13: K to last 4 sts, kfb, sl3 wyif. (*19 sts*)
Now work at outer edge of wing only.
Row 14: K3, wyib sl sts back to LH needle. Pull yarn across back of sts to start of row.
Rep last row once more.
Row 16: Knit.
Row 17: K to last 5 sts, k2tog, sl3 wyif. (*18 sts*)
Row 18: K to last 2 sts, kfb, k1. (*19 sts*)
Row 19: K to last 5 sts, k2tog, sl3 wyif. (*18 sts*)
Row 20: K to last 3 sts, k2tog, k1. (*17 sts*)
Rep last 2 rows once more. (*15 sts*)
Row 23: K1, ssk, k to last 5 sts, k2tog, sl3 wyif. (*13 sts*)
Row 24: K to last 3 sts, k2tog, k1. (*12 sts*)
Rep last 2 rows twice more. (*6 sts*)
Row 29: K1, k2tog, sl3 wyif. (*5 sts*)
Row 30: K2, k2tog, k1. (*4 sts*)
Row 31: K2, k2tog. (*2 sts*)
Bind (cast) off.
Thread yarn through rem st to fasten off.

Ear

(make two)
Using MC, cast on 4 sts.
Row 1 (RS): K1, M1, k2, M1, k1. (*6 sts*)
Starting with a p row, work 3 rows in st st.
Row 5: Ssk, k2, k2tog. (*4 sts*)
Row 6: P2tog, p2togtbl. (*2 sts*)
Lift second st on LH needle over first st to bind (cast) off, thread yarn through rem st and fasten off, leaving length of yarn for sewing up.

Leg strap

(make two)
Using DPNs and MC, cast on 2 sts.
Row 1: K2, push sts to other end of needle, pulling yarn firmly across back of work, without turning.
Rep Row 1 five times more.
Thread yarn through sts, leaving a length for sewing up.

Making up

Sew the seam from the base of the body to the bottom of the head, then stuff with toy filling. Sew the seam at the back of the head together. Add the safety eyes to the head by pushing through the knitting using the photos as a guide for position. When you are happy with the placement, firmly push the backs onto the post of each eye. Stuff the head with toy filling. When you are happy with the amount of toy filling inside the head, sew the seam at the top of the head closed. Repeat for the seam at the bottom of the body. Thread a length of MC through the stitches around the neck and tighten to give the neck more definition, then fasten off.

Using A, embroider the nose using straight stitches (see page 142).

Pin the wings in place on each side of the body, using the photo as a guide. Sew in place.

Sew the seam closed on the leg and foot and stuff with toy filling. The seam will face toward the back of the bat. Using the photos for guidance, pin each leg and foot in place. When you are happy with their placement, sew firmly in place.

With WS together fold the cast-on edge of the ear in half and sew together to give the ear its shape. Repeat for the second ear. Using the photo as a guide for position, pin the ears in place. When you are happy with their placement, sew in place.

Using matching sewing cotton, sew the small button behind the top edge of the right-hand wing. Using a length of MC, sew a loop lengthwise onto the back of the left wing, so that it lies behind the wing. The wing can now be folded over the front of the bat and attached using the button.

Catch stitch each leg strap in place at the top and bottom of the back of the leg to form a loop. You can now hang your bat upside down!

shadow the bat   115

Skill Level ★ ★ ★

tango the toucan

The toucan's body is knitted using the intarsia technique. The bright and cheerful beak is striped with a slipped stitch in the center to add definition. Did you know that toucans regulate the temperature of their bodies by adjusting how blood flows to their beaks?

Yarn and materials
Rico Ricorumi DK (100% cotton) light worsted (DK) weight yarn, 63yd (58m) per ⅞oz (25g) ball
1 ball of Black 060 (MC)
¾ ball in each of the following:
White 001 (A)
Aqua 074 (turquoise) (B)
Small amounts in each of the following:
Red 028 (C)
Orange 027 (D)
Tangerine 026 (dark yellow) (E)
Pair of 6mm black domed safety eyes

Toy filling

Needles and equipment
US 2 or 3 (3mm) knitting needles

US 2 or 3 (3mm) double-pointed needles (DPNs)

Yarn needle

Scissors

Pins

Finished size
Base to top of head: 6¾in (17cm)

Beak to tail: 7⅛in (18cm)

Gauge (tension)
Approx 26 sts to 4in (10cm) measured over stockinette (stocking) stitch using US 2 or 3 (3mm) knitting needles.

Abbreviations
See page 143.

Pattern note
Wind a separate small ball of MC before you begin, for the intarsia section on the body and head.

Body and head
Start at bottom of body.
Using MC, cast on 14 sts.
Row 1 (WS): Purl.
Next row is written out in full to show pattern of increases.
Row 2: K1, kfb, k1, kfb, kfb, k1, kfb, kfb, k1, kfb, kfb, k1, kfb, k1. *(22 sts)*
Row 3: Purl.
Row 4: K1, [kfb, k3, kfb] to last st, k1. *(30 sts)*
Row 5: Purl.
Row 6: K1, [kfb, k5, kfb] to last st, k1. *(38 sts)*
Row 7: Purl.
Row 8: K1, [kfb, k7, kfb] to last st, k1. *(46 sts)*
Row 9: Purl.
Row 10: K1, kfb, k20, [kfb] twice, k20, kfb, k1. *(50 sts)*
Row 11: Purl.
Row 12: K1, kfb, k22, [kfb] twice, k22, kfb, k1. *(54 sts)*
Starting with a p row, work 15 rows in st st.
Join in A and second mini ball of MC, working in intarsia (see page 141) cont as follows:
Row 28: Using MC, k25, using A, k4, using MC, k25.
Row 29: Using MC, p24, using A, p6, using MC, p24.
Row 30: Using MC, k23, using A, k8, using MC, k23.
Row 31: Using MC, p22, using A, p10, using MC, p22.
Row 32: Using MC, k21, using A, k12, using MC, k21.
Row 33: Using MC, p20, using A, p14, using MC, p20.
Row 34: Using MC, k19, using A, k16, using MC, k19.
Row 35: Using MC, p18, using A, p18, using MC, p18.
Row 36: Using MC, k17, using A, k20, using MC, k17.
Row 37: Using MC, p16, using A, p22, using MC, p16.
Row 38: Using MC, k8, turn.
Shaping is done with short rows (see page 140).
Row 39: Using MC, slds, p to end.
Row 40: Using MC, k4, turn.
Row 41: Using MC, slds, p to end.
Row 42: Using MC, bind (cast) off 10 sts, then k6, using A, k20, using MC, k17. *(44 sts)*
Row 43: Using MC, p8, turn.
Row 44: Using MC, slds, k to end.
Row 45: Using MC, p4, turn.

116 skies and trees

Row 46: Using MC, slds, k to end.
Row 47: Using MC, bind (cast) off 10 sts purlwise, then p5, using A, p22, using MC, p6. (*34 sts*)
Row 48: Using MC, k1, ssk, k2, using A, k24, using MC, k2, k2tog, k1. (*32 sts*)
Row 49: Using MC, p4, using A, p24, using MC, p4.
Row 50: Using MC, k4, using A, k24, using MC, k4.
Row 51: Using MC, p4, using A, p24, using MC, p4.
Rep Rows 50 and 51 seven more times.
Row 66: Using MC, k4, using A, k2tog, k20, ssk, using MC, k4. (*30 sts*)
Row 67: Using MC, p4, using A, p22, using MC, p4.
Row 68: Using MC, k4, using A, k2tog, k18, ssk, using MC, k4. (*28 sts*)
Row 69: Using MC, p4, using A, p2togtbl, p16, p2tog, using MC, p4. (*26 sts*)
Break off A and second ball of MC and cont using MC.
Row 70: K4, ssk, k14, k2tog, k4. (*24 sts*)
Row 71: P4, p2tog, p2, p2togtbl, p4, p2tog, p2, p2togtbl, p4. (*20 sts*)
Row 72: K1, ssk, k4, k2tog, k2, ssk, k4, k2tog, k1. (*16 sts*)
Row 73: P1, p2tog, p2, p2togtbl, p2, p2tog, p2, p2togtbl, p1. (*12 sts*)
Divide rem sts evenly between two needles and, with RS tog and using third needle, bind (cast) off using three-needle bind (cast) off technique (see page 139).

TIP When changing color on the beak, leave a longer length of yarn to sew each colored part together.

118 skies and trees

Beak

Using MC, cast on 18 sts.

Row 1: Knit.

Break off MC and change to C.

Starting with a p row, work 5 rows in st st.

Join in D.

Row 7: [K1 in D, k1 in C] to end of row.

Break off C and, starting with a p row, work 5 rows in st st.

Join in E.

Row 13: [K1 using E, k1 using D] to end of row.

Break off D and, starting with a p row, work 3 rows in st st.

Row 17: K7, k2tog, ssk, k7. (16 sts)

Row 18: P6, p2togtbl, p2tog, p6. (14 sts)

Row 19: K5, k2tog, ssk, k5. (12 sts)

Break off E and join in MC.

Row 20: K4, k2tog, ssk, k4. (10 sts)

Row 21: P3, p2togtbl, p2tog, p3. (8 sts)

Row 22: K2, k2tog, ssk, k2. (6 sts)

Divide rem sts evenly between two needles and, with RS tog and using third needle, bind (cast) off using three-needle bind (cast) off technique.

Left wing

*Using MC, cast on 5 sts.

Row 1: K1, M1, k to last st, M1, k1. (7 sts)

Row 2: Purl.

Row 3: K1, M1, k to last st, M1, k1. (9 sts)

Row 4: P1, M1, p to last st, M1, p1. (11 sts)

Rep Rows 1–4 once more. (17 sts)*

Row 9: K to last st, M1, k1. (18 sts)

Starting with a p row, work 7 rows in st st.

Row 17: K1, k2tog, k to end. (17 sts)

Row 18: Purl.

Rep last 2 rows once more. (16 sts)

Row 21: K1, k2tog, k to end. (15 sts)

Row 22: P to last 3 sts, p2tog, p1. (14 sts)

Rep Rows 21 and 22 three more times. (8 sts)

Bind (cast) off.

Right wing

Work as for left wing from * to *.

Row 9: K1, M1, k to end. (18 sts)

Starting with a p row, work 7 rows in st st.

Row 17: K to last 3 sts, ssk, k1. (17 sts)

Row 18: Purl.

Rep Rows 17 and 18 once more. (16 sts)

Row 21: K to last 3 sts, ssk, k1. (15 sts)

Row 22: P1, p2togtbl, p to end. (14 sts)

Rep Rows 21 and 22 three more times. (8 sts)

Bind (cast) off.

Leg and foot

(make two)

Using DPNs and B, cast on 4 sts.

Row 1: K4, push sts to other end of needle, pulling yarn firmly across back of work, without turning.

Rep Row 1 six more times.

Row 8: K1, M1, k to last st, M1, k1. (6 sts)

Row 9: Purl.

Rep Rows 8 and 9 four more times. (14 sts)

Starting with a k row, work 2 rows in st st.

Row 20: Purl (creates fold line).

Starting with a p row, work 3 rows in st st.

Row 24: K1, K2tog, k to last 3 sts, ssk, k1. (12 sts)

Row 25: Purl.

Rep Rows 24 and 25 three more times. (6 sts)

Row 32: K1, k2tog, ssk, k1. (4 sts)

Row 33: P2tog, p2togtbl. (2 sts)

Thread yarn through rem sts to fasten, leaving length of yarn for sewing up.

Making up

Pin the head together and stuff with toy filling. Using the photos for guidance, pin the beak in place temporarily. Push the safety eyes through the knitting and when you are happy with their placement, remove the pins, toy filling, and beak and firmly push the back onto the post of each eye. Starting at the base of the body, gather the cast-on edge and sew along the seam to the tail. Stuff the body with toy filling. Sew the seam across the back of the toucan, adding more toy filling as necessary and ensuring it is pushed into the tail. Continue sewing the seam along the neck, stuffing with toy filling as you go. Sew the top of the seam closed.

Sew the beak together, matching the colors as you go, and stuff with toy filling. Pin the beak in place so that the top of the beak is sewn to the lower edge of the black section on the top of the head.

Pin the wings in place each side of the body, using the photos for guidance. When you are happy they are level, sew in place from the top front edge, along the front, and round to the bottom of the bound- (cast-) off edge.

Fold the foot section at the purl ridge. Sew the first side seam on the leg and foot, stuff with a small amount of toy filling to add definition, then sew the second seam closed. Pin each leg and foot in place, using the photos as a guide for position. Sew in place.

tango the toucan 119

Skill Level ★ ★ ★

piper the pelican

The pelican's beak has slipped stitches at each side to add definition. He is joined by a little silver fish who is made using lurex yarn and slips inside his wing. As the saying goes, "a pelican can hold more in his beak than his belly can!"

Yarn and materials
Rico Ricorumi DK (100% cotton) light worsted (DK) weight yarn, 63yd (58m) per ⅞oz (25g) ball
   1 ball of White 001 (MC)
   ¼ ball of Black 060 (CC)
   ¾ ball of Saffron 063 (yellow) (A)

Rico Ricorumi Lamé DK (62% polyester, 38% polyamide) light worsted (DK) weight yarn, 63yd (50m) per ⅜oz (10g) ball
   Small amount of Silver 001 (gray) (B)

Pair of 6mm black domed safety eyes

Two 3mm seed beads

Toy filling

Needles and equipment
US 2 or 3 (3mm) knitting needles

US 2 or 3 (3mm) double-pointed needles (DPNs)

Yarn needle

Scissors

Pins

Finished size
Rear to tip of beak: 6¾in (17cm)

Top of head to foot: 9in (23cm)

Gauge (tension)
Approx 26 sts to 4in (10cm) measured over stockinette (stocking) stitch using US 2 or 3 (3mm) knitting needles.

Abbreviations
See page 143.

Body and head
Start at bottom of body.
Using MC, cast on 14 sts.
Row 1 (WS): Purl.
Next row is written out in full to show pattern of increases.
Row 2: K1, kfb, k1, kfb, kfb, k1, kfb, kfb, k1, kfb, kfb, k1, kfb, k1. (*22 sts*)
Row 3: Purl.
Row 4: K1, [kfb, k3, kfb] to last st, k1. (*30 sts*)
Row 5: Purl.
Row 6: K1, [kfb, k5, kfb] to last st, k1. (*38 sts*)
Row 7: Purl.
Row 8: K1, [kfb, k7, kfb] to last st, k1. (*46 sts*)
Row 9: Purl.
Row 10: K1, kfb, k20, [kfb] twice, k20, kfb, k1. (*50 sts*)
Row 11: Purl.
Row 12: K1, kfb, k22, [kfb] twice, k22, kfb, k1. (*54 sts*)
Starting with a p row, work 15 rows in st st.
Row 28: K26, [kfb] twice, k26. (*56 sts*)
Starting with a p row, work 3 rows in st st.
Row 32: K27, [kfb] twice, k27. (*58 sts*)
Starting with a p row, work 7 rows in st st.
Row 40: K26, ssk, k2, k2tog, k26. (*56 sts*)
Starting with a p row, work 3 rows in st st.
Row 44: Bind (cast) off 3 sts, then k21, ssk, k2, k2tog, k to end. (*51 sts*)
Row 45: Bind (cast) off 3 sts, p to end. (*48 sts*)
Row 46: Bind (cast) off 3 sts, k to end. (*45 sts*)
Row 47: Bind (cast) off 3 sts, p to end. (*42 sts*)
Row 48: Bind (cast) off 4 sts, then k13, ssk, k2, k2tog, k to end. (*36 sts*)
Row 49: Bind (cast) off 4 sts, p to end. (*32 sts*)
Row 50: Bind (cast) off 3 sts, k to end. (*29 sts*)
Row 51: Bind (cast) off 3 sts, p to end. (*26 sts*)
Row 52: K1, M1, k9, ssk, k2, k2tog, k9, M1, k1. (*26 sts*)
Starting with a p row, work 3 rows in st st.
Rep last 4 rows three more times.
Row 68: K1, ssk, k7, ssk, k2, k2tog, k7, k2tog, k1. (*22 sts*)
Row 69: Purl.
Row 70: K1, ssk, k5, ssk, k2, k2tog, k5, k2tog, k1. (*18 sts*)
Row 71: Purl.
Row 72: K1, ssk, k3, ssk, k2, k2tog, k3, k2tog, k1. (*14 sts*)

120   skies and trees

Row 73: Purl.
Divide rem sts evenly between two needles and, with RS tog and using third needle, bind (cast) off using three-needle bind (cast) off technique (see page 139).

Beak
Starting at inside edge of beak, worked in two halves.
FIRST HALF
*Using A, cast on 3 sts.
Row 1 (WS): Purl.
Row 2: [K1, M1] twice, k1. (*5 sts*)
Row 3: Purl.*
Cut yarn and place sts on spare needle.
SECOND HALF
Work from * to * once more.
Join halves.
Note: When working sl2, always slip sts purlwise to avoid twisting sts.
Row 4: K5 (across sts on needle), cast on 12 sts, k5 from spare needle. (*22 sts*)
Row 5: Purl.
Row 6: K1, M1, k5, sl2, k6, sl2, k5, M1, k1. (*24 sts*)
Row 7: Purl.
Row 8: K7, sl2, k6, sl2, k7.
Row 9: Purl.
Row 10: K1, M1, k6, sl2, k6, sl2, k6, M1, k1. (*26 sts*)
Row 11: Purl.
Row 12: K1, M1, k7, sl2, k6, sl2, k7, M1, k1. (*28 sts*)
Row 13: Purl.
Row 14: K9, sl2, k6, sl2, k9.
Row 15: Purl.
Rep last 2 rows three more times.
Row 22: K1, ssk, k6, sl2, k6, sl2, k6, k2tog, k1. (*26 sts*)
Row 23: Purl.
Row 24: K1, ssk, k5, sl2, k6, sl2, k5, k2tog, k1. (*24 sts*)
Row 25: Purl.
Row 26: K1, ssk, k4, sl2, ssk, k2, k2tog, sl2, k4, k2tog, k1. (*20 sts*)
Row 27: Purl.
Row 28: K1, ssk, k3, sl2, ssk, k2tog, sl2, k3, k2tog, k1. (*16 sts*)
Row 29: P1, p2tog, p to last 3 sts, p2togtbl, p1. (*14 sts*)
Row 30: K1, ssk, k1, sl2, k2, sl2, k1, k2tog, k1. (*12 sts*)
Row 31: P1, p2togtbl, p2, p2tog, p2, p2tog, p1. (*9 sts*)
Row 32: P1, [p2tog] four times. (*5 sts*)
Thread yarn through rem sts to fasten off, leaving length of yarn for sewing up.

Left wing
*Using MC, cast on 7 sts.
Row 1 (RS): K1, M1, k to last st, M1, k1. (*9 sts*)
Row 2: Purl.
Row 3: K1, M1, k to last st, M1, k1. (*11 sts*)
Row 4: P1, M1, p to last st, M1, p1. (*13 sts*)
Rep last 4 rows once more. (*19 sts*)
Starting with a k row, work 6 rows in st st.*
Row 15: K1, k2tog, k to end. (*18 sts*)
Row 16: Purl.
Row 17: K1, k2tog, k to end. (*17 sts*)
Row 18: P to last 3 sts, p2tog, p1. (*16 sts*)
Rep last 4 rows once more. (*13 sts*)
Change to CC.
Row 23: K1, k2tog, k to end. (*12 sts*)
Row 24: P to last 3 sts, p2tog, p1. (*11 sts*)
Row 25: K1, k2tog, k5, ssk, k1. (*9 sts*)
Row 26: P1, p2togtbl, p3, p2tog, p1. (*7 sts*)

122 skies and trees

Row 27: K1, k2tog, k1, ssk, k1. (*5 sts*)
Row 28: P2togtbl, p1, p2tog. (*3 sts*)
Row 29: CDD. (*1 st*)
Thread yarn through rem st to fasten off.

Right wing

Work as for left wing from * to *.
Row 15: K, k to last 3 sts, ssk, k1. (*18 sts*)
Row 16: Purl.
Row 17: K to last 3 sts, ssk, k1. (*17 sts*)
Row 18: P1, p2togtbl, p to end. (*16 sts*)
Rep last 4 rows once more.
Change to CC.
Row 23: K to last 3 sts, ssk, k1. (*12 sts*)
Row 24: P1, p2togtbl, p to end. (*11 sts*)
Row 25: K1, k2tog, k5, ssk, k1. (*9 sts*)
Row 26: P1, p2togtbl, p3, p2tog, p1. (*7 sts*)
Row 27: K1, k2tog, k1, ssk, k1. (*5 sts*)
Row 28: P2togtbl, p1, p2tog. (*3 sts*)
Row 29: CDD. (*1 sts*)
Thread yarn through rem st to fasten off.

Leg and foot

(make two)
Using A, cast on 4 sts.
Row 1: K4, push sts to other end of needle, pulling yarn firmly across back of work, without turning.
Rep Row 1 six more times.
Beg working flat.
Row 8: K1, M1, k to last st, M1, k1. (*6 sts*)
Row 9: Purl.
Rep last 2 rows four more times. (*14 sts*)
Starting with a k row, work 2 rows in st st.
Row 20: Purl (this row forms fold line).
Starting with a p row, work 3 rows in st st.
Row 24: K1, k2tog, k to last 3 sts, ssk, k1. (*12 sts*)
Row 25: Purl.
Rep last 2 rows three more times. (*6 sts*)
Row 32: K1, k2tog, ssk, k1. (*4 sts*)
Row 33: P2tog, p2togtbl. (*2 sts*)
Thread yarn through rem sts to fasten off, leaving length of yarn for sewing up.

Fish

Using B, cast on 2 sts.
Row 1: K1, M1, k1. (*3 sts*)
Row 2: Purl.
Row 3: [K1, M1] twice, k1. (*5 sts*)
Row 4: P1, M1, p3, M1, p1. (*7 sts*)
Starting with a k row, work 4 rows in st st.
Row 9: Ssk, k3, k2tog. (*5 sts*)
Row 10: P2tog, p1, p2togtbl. (*3 sts*)
Row 11: Knit.
Row 12: [P1, M1] twice, p1. (*5 sts*)
Row 13: K1, M1, k3, M1, k1. (*7 sts*)
Rows 14–16: Purl (Row 15 forms a fold line).

Row 17: Ssk, k3, k2tog. (*5 sts*)
Row 18: P2tog, p1, p2togtbl. (*3 sts*)
Row 19: Knit.
Row 20: [P1, M1] twice, p1. (*5 sts*)
Row 21: K1, M1, k3, M1, k1. (*7 sts*)
Starting with a p row, work 4 rows in st st.
Row 26: P2tog, p3, p2togtbl. (*5 sts*)
Row 27: Ssk, k1, k2tog. (*3 sts*)
Row 28: Purl.
Row 29: K2tog, k1. (*2 sts*)
Thread yarn through rem sts to fasten off, leaving length of yarn for sewing up.

Making up

Pin the head together and stuff with toy filling. Using the photos as a guide for position, pin the beak in place. Push the safety eyes through the knitting, again using the photos for position. When you are happy with their placement, remove the pins, beak, and toy filling and firmly push the back onto the post of each eye. Re-stuff the head.

Starting at the base of the body, gather the cast-on edge and sew along the seam to the tail. Stuff the body with toy filling. Sew the seam across the back of the pelican, adding more toy filling as necessary and ensuring it is pushed into the tail. Continue sewing the seam along the neck, stuffing with toy filling as you go. Sew the top of the seam closed.

Sew the beak together, stuffing with toy filling. Pin the beak in place again. Pin the wings in place each side of the body. When you are happy they are level, sew in place along the front curved edge, changing to CC to sew the back of the wing in place. Sew along the top edge to where CC meets MC.

On each leg and foot fold over at the fold line, sew the first foot side seam, stuff with a small amount of toy filling to add definition, then sew the second seam closed. Pin each foot in place, using the photos for guidance and with the bound- (cast-) off edge of the foot underneath. Sew in place.

Fold the fish in half along the fold line and sew together, placing a small amount of toy filling inside. Sew the seed beads in place as eyes.

TIP Pin the wings in place before sewing them on, and to check they are level, look from the front, back, and top of the bird.

Skill Level ★ ★ ★

apollo the owl

This lovely little owl's face is knitted in two halves and sewn together, and the feet are made of three knitted bobbles worked in a row. Did you know that owls can rotate their necks 270 degrees but can't move their eyes?

Yarn and materials
Rowan Alpaca Classic (57% alpaca, 43% cotton) light worsted (DK) weight yarn, 131yd (120m) per ⅞oz (50g) ball
  ¾ ball of shade Snowflake White 115 (MC)

Rowan Felted Tweed (50% wool, 25% viscose, 25% alpaca) light worsted (DK) weight yarn, 191yd (175m) per 1¾oz (50g) ball
  ½ ball of Scree 165 (gray) (CC1)
  Small amount of Camel 157 (light brown) (CC2)

Pair of 6mm black domed safety eyes

Toy filling

Needles and equipment
US 2 or 3 (3mm) knitting needles

US 2 or 3 (3mm) double-pointed needles (DPNs)

Stitch markers

Yarn needle

Scissors

Pins

Finished size
Head to toe: 6¼in (16cm)

Gauge (tension)
Approx 26 sts to 4in (10cm) measured over stockinette (stocking) stitch using US 2 or 3 (3mm) knitting needles.

Abbreviations
See page 143.

Pattern note
Wind a separate small ball of CC1 before you begin, for the intarsia section on the body and head.

Face
Worked in two halves.
FIRST EYE SECTION
Using CC1, cast on 25 sts.
Row 1: Knit.
Break off CC1, join in MC.
Shaping is done with short rows (see page 140).
Row 2: P23, turn.
Row 3: Slds, k13, turn.
Row 4: Slds, p12, turn.
Row 5: Slds, k7, turn.
Row 6: Slds, p to end.
Row 7: [K3, k2tog] 5 times. (*20 sts*)
Row 8: Purl.
Row 9: [K2, k2tog] 5 times. (*15 sts*)
Row 10: Purl.
Row 11: [K1, k2tog] 5 times. (*10 sts*)
Row 12: Purl.
Row 13: [K2tog] five times. (*5 sts*)
Thread yarn through rem sts.
SECOND EYE SECTION
Using CC1, cast on 25 sts.
Row 1: Knit.
Break off CC1, join in MC.
Shaping is done with short rows.
Row 2: P16, turn.
Row 3: Slds, k12, turn.
Row 4: Slds, p7, turn.
Row 5: Slds, k6, turn.
Row 6: Slds, p to end.
Work as for Rows 7–13 of first eye section.
Thread yarn through rem sts.

124 skies and trees

Body and head

Start at base.
Using MC, cast on 12 sts.
Row 1 (WS): Purl.
Row 2: K2, M1, k to last 2 sts, M1, k2. (*14 sts*)
Row 3: Purl.
Row 4: K2, M1, k to last 2 sts, M1, k2. (*16 sts*)
Row 5: P2, M1, p to last 2 sts, M1, p2. (*18 sts*)
Row 6: K2, M1, k to last 2 sts, M1, k2. (*20 sts*)
Row 7: Purl.
Row 8: K2, M1, k to last 2 sts, M1, k2. (*22 sts*)
Row 9: P2, M1, p to last 2 sts, M1, p2. (*24 sts*)
Row 10: K2, M1, k to last 2 sts, M1, k2. (*26 sts*)
Row 11: Purl.
Row 12: Knit.
Row 13: Purl.
Rep Rows 12 and 13 four more times.
Row 22: K2, ssk, k to last 4 sts, k2tog, k2. (*24 sts*)
Row 23: P2, p2tog, p to last 4 sts, p2togtbl, p2. (*22 sts*)
Rep Rows 22 and 23 once more. (*18 sts*)
Break MC, join in strand of CC1, and work in intarsia (see page 141).
Row 26: Using CC1, cast on 18 sts, working across these sts k18, rejoin MC, k18. (*36 sts*)
Join in separate strand of CC1.
Row 27: Using CC1, cast on 18 sts, working across these sts p18, using MC, p18, using CC1, p18. (*54 sts*)
Row 28: Using CC1, k18, using MC, k6, M1, k6, M1, k6, using CC1, k18. (*56 sts*)
Row 29: Using CC1, p18, using MC, p20, using CC1, p18.
Row 30: Using CC1, k18, using MC, k7, M1, k6, M1, k7, using CC1, k18. (*58 sts*)
Row 31: Using CC1, p18, using MC, p22, using CC1, p18.
Row 32: Using CC1, k18, using MC, k8, M1, k6, M1, k8, using CC1, k18. (*60 sts*)
Row 33: Using CC1, p18, using MC, p24, using CC1, p18.
Row 34: Using CC1, k18, using MC, k24, using CC1, k18.
Row 35: Using CC1, p18, using MC, p24, using CC1, p18.
Rep Rows 34 and 35 ten more times.
Row 56: Using CC1, k18, using MC, k7, ssk, k6, k2tog, k7, using CC1, k18. (*58 sts*)
Row 57: Using CC1, p18, using MC, p22, using CC1, p18.
Row 58: Using CC1, k18, using MC, k6, ssk, k6, k2tog, k6, using CC1, k18. (*56 sts*)
Row 59: Using CC1, p18, using MC, p20, using CC1, p18.
Row 60: Using CC1, k6, ssk, k2, k2tog, k6, using MC, k5, ssk, k6, k2tog, k6, using CC1, k6, ssk, k2, k2tog, k6. (*50 sts*)
Row 61: Using CC1, p16, using MC, p18, using CC1, p16.
Row 62: Using CC1, k5, ssk, k2, k2tog, k5, using MC, k18, using CC1, k5, ssk, k2, k2tog, k5. (*36 sts*)
Row 63: Using CC1, p14, using MC, p18, using CC1, p14.
Row 64: Using CC1, k5, M1, k2, M1, k6, using MC, k18, using CC1, k6, M1, k2, M1, k6. (*40 sts*)
Row 65: Using CC1, p16, using MC, p18, using CC1, p16.
Row 66: Using CC1, k16, using MC, k18, using CC1, k16.
Row 67: Using CC1, p16, using MC, p18, using CC1, p16.

Rep Rows 66 and 67 three more times.
Row 74: Using CC1, k2, ssk, k12, using MC, ssk, k14, k2tog, using CC1, k12, k2tog, k2. (*46 sts*)
Row 75: Using CC1, p15, using MC, p16, using CC1, p15.
Row 76: Using CC1, k2, ssk, k11, using MC, ssk, k12, k2tog, using CC1, k11, k2tog, k2. (*42 sts*)
Row 77: Using CC1, p2, p2tog, p10, using MC, p2tog, p10, p2togtbl, using CC1, p10, p2togtbl, p2. (*38 sts*)
Row 78: Using CC1, k2, ssk, k7, k2tog, using MC, ssk, k8, k2tog, using CC1, ssk, k7, k2tog, k2. (*32 sts*)
Row 79: Using CC1, p2, p2tog, p5, p2togtbl, using MC, p2tog, p6, p2togtbl, using CC1, p2tog, p5, p2togtbl, p2. (*26 sts*)
Break off CC1, cont in MC.
Row 80: K4, ssk, k3, ssk, k4, k2tog, k3, k2tog, k4. (*22 sts*)
Row 81: Purl.
Bind (cast) off.

Wing

(make 2)
Worked in two halves.
FIRST SIDE
Using CC1, cast on 8 sts.
Row 1 (RS): Knit.
Row 2: Purl.
Row 3: K1, M1, k to last st, M1, k1. (*10 sts*)
Row 4: Purl.
Rep Rows 1–4 four more times. (*18 sts*)
Starting with a k row, work 16 rows in st st.
Row 37: K1, ssk, k to end. (*17 sts*)
Row 38: Purl.
Row 39: K1, ssk, k to end. (*16 sts*)
Row 40: P to last 3 sts, p2togtbl, p1. (*15 sts*)
Rep Rows 39 and 40 twice more. (*11 sts*)
Bind (cast) off.

SECOND SIDE
Work as for first side from Rows 1–36.
Row 37: K to last 3 sts, k2tog, k1. (*17 sts*)
Row 38: Purl.
Row 39: K to last 3 sts, k2tog, k1. (*16 sts*)
Row 40: P1, p2tog, p to end. (*15 sts*)
Rep last 2 rows twice more. (*11 sts*)
Bind (cast) off.

Tail
Using MC, cast on 14 sts.
Starting with a k row, work 4 rows in st st.
Row 5: K1, ssk, k to last 3 sts, k2tog, k1. (*12 sts*)
Row 6: Purl.
Rep last 2 rows three more times. (*6 sts*)
Change to CC1.
Row 13: Knit.
Row 14: Purl.
Row 15: K1, M1, k to last st, M1, k1. (*8 sts*)
Row 16: Purl.
Row 17: K2, M1, k to last 2 sts, M1, k2. (*10 sts*)
Row 18: Purl.
Rep Rows 17 and 18 three more times. (*16 sts*)
Bind (cast) off.

Beak
Using CC2, cast on 6 sts.
Row 1 (WS): Purl.
Shaping is done with short rows.
Row 2: K5, turn.
Row 3: Slds, p3, turn.
Row 4: Slds, k to end.
Row 5: Purl.
Row 6: Ssk, k2, k2tog. (*4 sts*)
Row 7: Purl.
Row 8: Ssk, k2tog. (*2 sts*)
Thread yarn through rem sts to fasten off.

Foot
(make 2)
Using CC2, cast on 1 st.
Row 1: Kfb. (*3 sts*)
Row 2: Purl.
Row 3: [K1, M1] twice, k1. (*5 sts*)
Row 4: Purl.
Row 5: Ssk, k1, k2tog. (*3 sts*)
Row 6: CDD. (*1 st*)
Rep Rows 1–6 twice more.
Bind (cast) off rem st.

Making up
Using matching yarn, and starting at the top of the head, sew the seam closed to the bottom edge of the body. Stuff with toy filling, leaving the bottom seam open.

Sew the eye sections together along the center seam with the shaped edge at the top, so you get a "heart" shape here on the face. Pin the face to the body. Add the safety eyes to the head by pushing through the knitting using the photos as a guide for position. When you are happy with the placement, firmly push the backs onto the post of each eye. Re-stuff the body and sew the base in place. Sew the face in place, removing the pins. Sew the first and second sides of the wing together. Repeat for the second wing. Pin the wings in place using the photos as a guide for position and sew in place along the top and bottom edge.

Gather the bound- (cast-) off edge of the beak and sew the seam that will be on the inside. Sew the beak to the front of the face, using the photos for guidance.

Sew each "bobble" on the foot closed then repeat for the second foot. Pin the feet in place and sew to the base of the body.

apollo the owl

Skill Level ★★★

binky the parrot

This little parrot is full of character. Her wings and tail are knitted in three colors, and the black face markings are embroidered on after she has been sewn together.

Yarn and materials
Rico Ricorumi DK (100% cotton) light worsted (DK) weight yarn, 63yd (58m) per ⅞oz (25g) ball
  1 ball each of:
    Sky Blue 031 (A)
    Saffron 063 (yellow) (B)
  ¾ ball each of:
    Black 060 (C)
    White 001 (D)
    Red 028 (E)
    Mouse Gray 059 (F)
Toy filling

Pair of 6mm black domed safety eyes

Needles and equipment
US 2 or 3 (3mm) knitting needles
US 2 or 3 (3mm) double-pointed needles (DPNs)
Yarn needle
Scissors
Pins

Finished size
Height: 6¾in (17cm)

Gauge (tension)
Approx 26 sts to 4in (10cm) measured over stockinette (stocking) stitch using US 2 or 3 (3mm) knitting needles.

Abbreviations
See page 143.

Pattern note
Most of the parrot is worked in intarsia, so wind several small balls of each color before you begin.

Body and head
Start at bottom of body. Using A, cast on 14 sts.
Row 1: Purl.
Next row is written out in full to show pattern of increases.
Row 2: K1, kfb, k1, kfb, kfb, k1, kfb, kfb, k1, kfb, kfb, k1, kfb, k1. (*22 sts*)
Row 3: Purl.
Row 4: K1, [kfb, k3, kfb] to last st, k1. (*30 sts*)
Row 5: Purl.
Row 6: K1, [kfb, k5, kfb] to last st, k1. (*38 sts*)
Row 7: Purl.
Row 8: K1, [kfb, k7, kfb] to last st, k1. (*46 sts*)
Row 9: Purl.
Row 10: K1, [kfb, k9, kfb] to last st, k1. (*54 sts*)
Row 11: Purl.
Join in B.
Row 12: Using B, k3, using A, k23, M1, k2, M1, k23, using B, K3. (*56 sts*)
Row 13: Using B, p5, using A, p46, using B, p5.
Row 14: Using B, k7, using A, k20, M1, k2, M1, k20, using B, k7. (*58 sts*)
Row 15: Using B, p9, using A, p40, using B, p9.
Row 16: Using B, k11, using A, k36, using B, k11.
Row 17: Using B, p13, using A, p32, using B, p13.
Row 18: Using B, k15, using A, k28, using B, k15.
Row 19: Using B, p15, using A, p28, using B, p15.
Row 20: Using B, k2, ssk, k11, using A, k28, using B, k11, k2tog, k2. (*56 sts*)
Row 21: Using B, p14, using A, p28, using B, p14.
Row 22: Using B, k14, using A, k28, using B, k14.
Row 23: Using B, p14, using A, p28, using B, p14.
Row 24: Using B, k2, ssk, k10, using A, k28, using B, k10, k2tog, k2. (*54 sts*)

Row 25: Using B, p13, using A, p28, using B, p13.
Row 26: Using B, k13, using A, k28, using B, k13.
Row 27: Using B, p13, using A, p28, using B, p13.
Row 28: Using B, k2, ssk, k9, using A, k28, using B, k9, k2tog, k2. (*52 sts*)
Row 29: Using B, p12, using A, p28, using B, p12.
Row 30: Using B, k12, using A, k28, using B, k12.
Row 31: Using B, p12, using A, p28, using B, p12.
Row 32: Using B, k2, ssk, k8, using A, k9, ssk, k6, k2tog, k9, using B, k8, k2tog, k2. (*48 sts*)
Row 33: Using B, p11, using A, p26, using B, p11.
Row 34: Using B, k11, using A, k26, using B, k11.
Row 35: Using B, p11, using A, p26, using B, p11.
Row 36: Using B, k2, ssk, k7, using A, k8, ssk, k6, k2tog, k8, using B, k7, k2tog, k2. (*44 sts*)
Row 37: Using B, p10, using A, p24, using B, p10.
Row 38: Using B, k11, using A, k6, ssk, k6, k2tog, k6, using B, k11. (*42 sts*)
Row 39: Using B, p12, using A, p18, using B, p12.
Row 40: Using B, k2, ssk, k9, using A, k3, ssk, k6, k2tog, k3, using B, k9, k2tog, k2. (*38 sts*)
Row 41: Using B, p13, using A, p12, using B, p13.
Break off A.
Row 42: Using B, k13, join in C, k1, ssk, k6, k2tog, k1, using B, k13. (*36 sts*)
Row 43: Using B, p12, using C, p12, using B, p12.
Row 44: Using B, k2, ssk, k8, using C, k12, using B, k8, k2tog, k2. (*34 sts*)
Row 45: Using B, p12, using C, p10, using B, p12.
Break off C.
Row 46: Using B, k10, join in D, using D, k14, using B, k10.
Row 47: Using B, p9, using D, p16, using B, p9.

binky the parrot 129

Row 48: Using B, k8, using D, k18, using B, k8.
Row 49: Using B, p7, using D, p20, using B, p7.
Row 50: Using B, k7, using D, k20, using B, k7.
Row 51: Using B, p7, using D, p20, using B, p7.
Rep last 2 rows twice more.
Row 56: Using B, k7, using D, k20, using B, k7.
Row 57: Using B, p8, using D, p18, using B, p8.
Row 58: Using B, k2, ssk, k5, using D, k16, using B, k5, k2tog, k2. (*32 sts*)
Row 59: Using B, p9, using D, p14, using B, p9.
Break off D, cont using B.
Row 60: K2, ssk, k24, k2tog, k2. (*30 sts*)
Row 61: Purl.
Row 62: K2, ssk, k8, k2tog, k2, ssk, k8, k2tog, k2. (*26 sts*)
Row 63: Purl.
Row 64: K2, ssk, k6, k2tog, k2, ssk, k6, k2tog, k2. (*22 sts*)
Row 65: P2, p2tog, p4, p2togtbl, p2, p2tog, p4, p2togtbl, p2. (*18 sts*)
Divide rem sts evenly between two needles and, with RS tog and using third needle, bind (cast) off using three-needle bind (cast) off technique (see page 139).

Wing side 1

(make two)
Using E, cast on 4 sts.
Row 1 (RS): Knit.
Row 2: Purl.
Row 3: K1, M1, k to last st, M1, k1. (*6 sts*)
Row 4: Purl.
Rep last 2 rows four more times. (*14 sts*)
Join in A.
Row 13: Using A, k2, using E, k12.
Row 14: Using E, p10, using A, p4.
Row 15: Using A, k1, M1, k5, using E, k7, M1, k1. (*16 sts*)
Row 16: Using E, p7, using A, p9.
Row 17: Using A, k11, using E, k5.
Row 18: Using E, p3, using A, p13.
Row 19: Using A, k1, M1, k14, using E, M1, k1. (*18 sts*)
Break off E.
Cont in A and starting with a p row, work 7 rows in st st.
Join in B.
Row 27: Using B, k2, using A, k16.
Row 28: Using A, p14, using B, p4.
Row 29: Using B, k6, using A, k12.
Row 30: Using A, p10, using B, p8.
Row 31: Using B, k1, ssk, k7, using A, k5, k2tog, k1. (*16 sts*)
Row 32: Using A, p5, using B, p11.
Row 33: Using B, k1, ssk, k10, using A, k2tog, k1. (*14 sts*)
Break off A, cont in B.
Row 34: Purl.
Row 35: K1, ssk, k to last 3 sts, k2tog, k1. (*12 sts*)
Row 36: Purl.
Row 37: K1, ssk, k to last 3 sts, k2tog, k1. (*10 sts*)
Row 38: P1, p2tog, p to last 3 sts, p2tog, p1. (*8 sts*)
Rep last 2 rows once more. (*4 sts*)
Bind (cast) off.

Wing side 2

(make two)
Using E, cast on 4 sts.
Row 1 (RS): Knit.
Row 2: Purl.
Row 3: K1, M1, k to last st, M1, k1. (*6 sts*)
Row 4: Purl.
Rep last 2 rows four more times. (*14 sts*)
Row 13: Using E, k12, using A, k2.
Row 14: Using A, p14, using E, p10.
Row 15: Using E, k1, M1, k7, using A, k5, M1, k1. (*16 sts*)
Row 16: Using A, p9, using E, p7.
Row 17: Using E, k5, using A, k11.
Row 18: Using A, p13, using E, p3.
Row 19: Using E, k1, M1, using A, k14, M1, k1. (*18 sts*)
Break off E.
Cont in A, and starting with a p row, work 7 rows in st st.
Join in B.
Row 27: Using A, k16, using B, k2.
Row 28: Using B, p4, using A, p14.
Row 29: Using A, k12, using B, k6.
Row 30: Using B, p8, using A, p10.
Row 31: Using A, k1, k2tog, k5, using B, k7, ssk, k1. (*16 sts*)
Row 32: Using B, p11, using A, p5.
Row 33: Using A, k1, k2tog, using B, k10, ssk, k1. (*14 sts*)
Break off A, cont in B.
Row 34: Purl.
Row 35: K1, ssk, k to last 3 sts, k2tog, k1. (*12 sts*)
Row 36: Purl.
Row 37: K1, ssk, k to last 3 sts, k2tog, k1. (*10 sts*)
Row 38: P1, p2tog, p to last 3 sts, p2togtbl, p1. (*8 sts*)
Rep last 2 rows once more. (*4 sts*)
Bind (cast) off.

Tail

Using A, cast on 5 sts.
Work slipped sts purlwise to avoid them twisting.
Row 1 (RS): K2, sl1, k2.
Row 2: Purl.
Row 3: K1, M1, k1, sl1, k1, M1, k1. (*7 sts*)
Row 4: Purl.
Row 5: K3, sl1, k3.
Row 6: Purl.
Row 7: K1, M1, k2, sl1, k2, M1, k1. (*9 sts*)
Row 8: Purl.
Row 9: K4, sl1, k4.
Row 10: Purl.
Break off A, cont in E.
Row 11: K1, M1, k3, sl1, k3, M1, k1. (*11 sts*)
Row 12: Purl.
Row 13: K5, sl1, k5.
Row 14: Purl.
Row 15: K1, M1, k4, sl1, k4, M1, k1. (*13 sts*)
Row 16: Purl.
Row 17: K6, sl1, k6.
Row 18: Purl.
Row 19: K1, M1, k5, sl1, k5, M1, k1. (*15 sts*)

Row 20: Purl.
Row 21: K7, sl1, k7.
Row 22: Purl.
Break off E, cont in B.
Row 23: K1, M1, k6, sl1, k6, M1, k1. (*17 sts*)
Row 24: Purl.
Row 25: K8, sl1, k8.
Row 26: Purl.
Row 27: K1, M1, k7, sl1, k7, M1, k1. (*19 sts*)
Row 28: Purl.
Row 29: K9, sl1, k9.
Row 30: Purl.
Bind (cast) off.

Beak

Using D, cast on 18 sts.
Starting with a k row, work 2 rows in st st.
Break off D, join in F.
Starting with a k row, work 4 rows in st st.
Shaping is done with short rows (see page 140).
Row 7: K13, turn.
Row 8: Slds, p7, turn.
Row 9: Slds, k9, turn.
Row 10: Slds, p11, turn.
Row 11: Slds, k13, turn.
Row 12: Slds, p15, turn.
Row 13: Slds, k to end.
Row 14: P7, p2tog, p2togtbl, p7. (*16 sts*)
Row 15: K2, k2tog, k1, ssk, k2, k2tog, k1, ssk, k2. (*12 sts*)
Row 16: P2, p2tog, p4, p2togtbl, p2. (*10 sts*)
Row 17: [K2tog] 5 times. (*5 sts*)
Row 18: Purl.
Thread yarn through rem sts to fasten off.

Foot and leg

(make two)
*Using F and DPNs, cast on 2 sts.
Row 1 (WS): Purl.
Row 2: K1, M1, k1. (*3 sts*)
Row 3: K3, push sts to other end of needle, pulling yarn firmly across back of work, without turning.
Rep Row 3 once.
Break off yarn, leave sts on spare needle.*
Work from * to * once more, then work from * to **.
Now working to end and across other two toes on spare needle, with RS facing join toes as foll:
Row 1: Cast on 2 sts, k2, [k2tog] 4 times, k1. (*7 sts*)
Row 2: Cast on 2 sts, p2, [p2tog] 3 times, p1. (*6 sts*)
Break F, join in A.
Row 3: Knit.
Row 4: [P1, M1] 5 times, p1. (*11 sts*)
Starting with a k row, work 2 rows in st st.
Row 7: [K1, M1] 10 times, k1. (*21 sts*)
Row 8: Purl.
Row 9: [K1, M1] 20 times, k1. (*41 sts*)
Row 10: Purl.
Bind (cast) off.

Making up

Pin the head together and stuff with toy filling. Add the safety eyes to the head by pushing through the knitting using the photos as a guide for position. When you are happy with the placement, remove the pins and toy filling and firmly push the backs onto the post of each eye. Re-stuff the head.

Starting at the top of the head, sew along the seam to the base of the body, stuffing with toy filling as you go. Gather the cast-on edge and close.

Join the seam of the beak. Stuff with toy filling. Pin the beak in place on the front of the face with the seam underneath, using the photos as a guide for position, then sew in place.

Sew a wing 1 to a wing 2 with WS together, matching the yarn colors as you go. Repeat for the second wing. Pin each wing in place following the photos for guidance. When you are happy they are level, using B join the outer edge of the top B section of the wing to the body. Repeat for the second wing.

Sew the foot together, continuing to sew the leg together adding some stuffing as you go. Pin each leg in position, and sew when you are happy with the placement.

Sew the seam from the tip of the tail to the base, using matching colors and stuffing with toy filling as you go. Sew in place using the photos as a guide for position.

Using C, embroider short stripes to each side of the face using two or three chain stitches (see page 142) as shown in the photos.

binky the parrot 131

techniques

Holding the needles
If you are a knitting novice, you will need to work out which is the most comfortable way for you to hold your needles.

Like a knife
Pick up the needles, one in each hand, as if you were holding a knife and fork—that is to say, with your hand lightly over the top of each needle. As you knit, you will tuck the blunt end of the right-hand needle under your arm, let go with your hand, and use your hand to manipulate the yarn, returning your hand to the needle to move the stitches along.

Like a pen
Now try changing the right hand so you are holding the needle as you would hold a pen, with your thumb and forefinger lightly gripping the needle close to its pointed tip and the shaft resting in the crook of your thumb. As you knit, you will not need to let go of the needle but simply slide your right hand forward to manipulate the yarn.

Holding the yarn
As you knit, you will be working stitches off the left-hand needle and onto the right needle, and the yarn you are working with needs to be tensioned and manipulated to produce an even fabric. To hold and tension the yarn, you can use either your right or left hand, depending on the method you are going to use to make the stitches.

Yarn in right hand
To knit and purl in the US/UK style (see pages 134 and 135), hold the yarn in your right hand. There are two ways of doing this.

Yarn in left hand
To knit and purl in the Continental style (see pages 135 and 136), hold the yarn in your left hand. This method is also sometimes easier for left-handed people to use.

To hold the yarn tightly, wind it right around your little finger, under your ring and middle fingers, then pass it over your index finger, which will manipulate the yarn.

For a looser hold, catch the yarn between your little and ring fingers, pass it under your middle finger, then over your index finger.

To hold the yarn tightly, wind it right around your little finger, under your ring and middle fingers, then pass it over your index finger, which will manipulate the yarn.

For a looser hold, fold your little, ring, and middle fingers over the yarn, and wind it twice around your index finger.

Cast on

Making a slip knot
A slip knot is the first loop that you put onto the needle to begin casting on in knitting.

1 Make a slip knot by winding the yarn twice around the first two fingers of your left hand, then bend these fingers forward. Draw the rear thread through the front one to form a loop.

2 With the knitting needle in your right hand, slide the loop onto the needle. Remove your fingers, then pull the two ends to tighten the loop on the needle and create the first stitch. Keep the needle with the slip knot in your left hand.

Cable method
This method makes a firm edge and uses two needles. It is given for the US/UK method of knitting here.

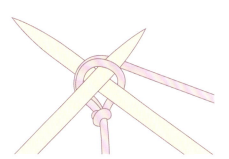  

1 First make a slip knot. Keep the yarn at the back and insert the right needle into the slip knot, from front to back, as shown in the illustration. Wrap the yarn from the ball end around the tip of the right needle and pull downward gently on it.

2 Draw the tip of the right needle through the loop and, as you do so, nudge the yarn through the loop of the slip knot to make a new loop. Turn the needle a little and slip this new loop onto the left needle, in front of the slip knot, and off the right needle. You now have two stitches.

3 Now insert the tip of the right needle between the two stitches on the left needle. Wrap the yarn over the right needle, from left to right. Now draw the yarn through to form a loop as you did before, then transfer it to the left needle and off the right, as you did in step 2. Repeat step 3 until you have created the desired number of stitches.

techniques 133

Applied i-cord cast on

This cast-on technique starts with making an i-cord and creates a rounded edge at the start of your piece.

1 Using double-pointed needles, cast on three stitches. Follow steps 1–2 on page 140 to make an i-cord that is as many rows as you want your project to be wide.

2 Slide the three stitches to the end of your needle and knit the three stitches together (see below and opposite).

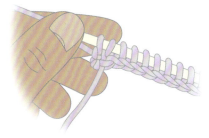

3 Using a crochet hook, pick up one stitch from the first "V" of the i-cord. Make sure you go underneath both "legs" of the stitch. Slip the loop onto your needle. Continue, picking up a stitch from each "V" of the i-cord and making sure the i-cord doesn't twist around.

4 When you reach the end of the i-cord, make sure you pick up a stitch through the very first row of the i-cord.

Knit stitch

There are only two stitches to master in knitting: knit and purl. Likewise, there are two main styles of knitting: the UK/US style and a method referred to as Continental style.

US/UK method

Place the needle with the cast-on stitches in your left hand and the empty needle in your right. Thread your yarn around your right hand, as shown on page 132.

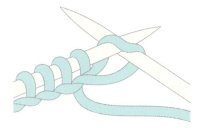

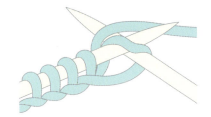

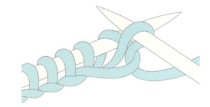

1 Hold the needle with the cast-on stitches in your left hand and the empty needle in your right hand. * From left to right, put the point of the right-hand needle into the front of the first stitch. Wrap the yarn around the point of the right-hand needle, again from left to right.

2 With the tip of the right-hand needle, pull the wrapped yarn through the stitch to form a loop. This loop is the new stitch.

3 Slip the original stitch off the left-hand needle by gently pulling the right-hand needle to the right. Repeat from * until you have knitted all the stitches on the left-hand needle. Swap the needles in your hands and you are ready to work the next row.

4 With the tip of the right needle, moving it to the right, push the stitch just worked off the tip of the left needle and gently tighten the new loop that now sits on the right needle. This is the first knit stitch. Repeat steps 1–3 for each stitch on the left needle, until this needle is empty.

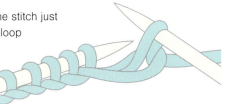

Continental method

This is how to form a knit stitch if you are holding the yarn in your left hand and so working in the Continental style. If you are left-handed, you may find this method easier than the US/UK technique (see opposite).

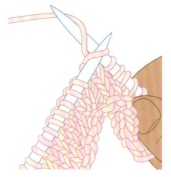 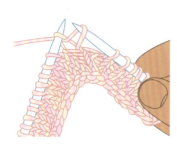 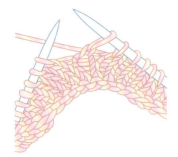

1 Hold the needle with the cast-on stitches in your left hand and the empty needle in your right hand. * From left to right, put the point of the right-hand needle into the front of the first stitch. Holding the working yarn fairly taut with your left hand at the back of the work, move the tip of the right-hand needle under the working yarn.

2 With the tip of the right-hand needle, bring the wrapped yarn through the stitch to form a loop. This loop is the new stitch.

3 Slip the original stitch off the left-hand needle by gently pulling the right-hand needle to the right. Repeat from * until you have knitted all the stitches on the left-hand needle. Swap the needles in your hands and you are ready to work the next row.

Purl

As with knit stitch, purl stitch can be formed in two ways. If you are new to knitting, try both techniques to see which works better for you: left-handed knitters may find the Continental method easier to master.

US/UK method

1 Hold the needle with the stitches in your left hand, and then insert the point of the right-hand needle into the front of the first stitch from right to left. Wind the yarn around the point of the right-hand needle, from right to left.

2 With the tip of the right-hand needle, pull the yarn through the stitch to form a loop. This loop is the new stitch.

3 Slip the original stitch off the left-hand needle by gently pulling the right-hand needle to the right. Repeat these steps until you have purled all the stitches on the left-hand needle. To work the next row, transfer the needle with all the stitches into your left hand.

techniques 135

Continental method

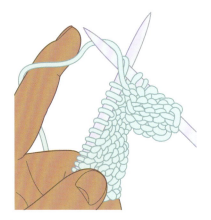

1 Place the needle containing all the stitches in your left hand and insert the tip of the right needle into the front of the first stitch, from right to left.

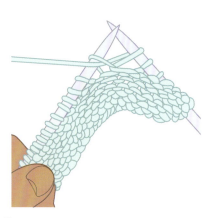

2 Hold the yarn at the back of the work, and keep it quite taut, but not tight. Pick up a loop of yarn with the tip of the right needle.

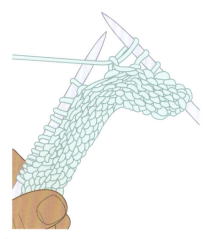

3 Use the tip of the right needle to draw this loop through the original stitch. This may feel trickier than making a knit stitch, but it is easy once you get used to the movements. Slip the original stitch off the left needle by moving the right needle gently to the right. Repeat steps 1–3 until all the stitches on the left needle have been used up.

Stockinette (stocking) stitch

To create this stitch, you work a row by knitting every stitch and then in the next row you purl every stitch. This makes a fabric with smooth V stitches (the knit stitches) on the right side of the fabric, and textured horizontal bars (the purl stitches) on the wrong side.

Reverse stockinette (stocking) stitch

This is created in the same way as stockinette (stocking) stitch above, except you start by working a row purling every stitch and then in the next row you knit every stitch. It creates a fabric with textured horizontal bars (the purl stitches) on the right side of the fabric, and smooth V stitches (the knit stitches) on the wrong side.

Slipping stitches (sl st)

Sometimes it is necessary to move a stitch from one needle to the other without working a stitch into it—this is known as slipping a stitch and is a very simple technique.

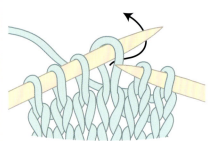

1 To slip a stitch knitwise, insert your right needle into the next stitch as if you were about to knit it, but instead of then wrapping the yarn, simply transfer the stitch off the left needle and onto the right one, without making a stitch. The yarn remains behind the work and is treated as normal for the following stitch.

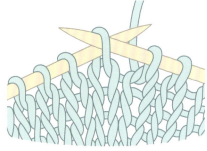

2 To slip a stitch purlwise, insert your right needle into the next stitch as if you were about to purl it, with the yarn at the front unless otherwise instructed. Instead of wrapping the yarn, simply transfer the stitch off the left needle and onto the right one, without making a stitch.

Increasing

Make 1 (M1)
This method can also be abbreviated as "M1l" (make 1 left). If a pattern just says "M1," this is the increase it refers to. It creates an extra stitch almost invisibly.

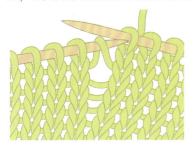 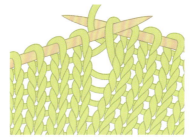 

1 From the front, slip the tip of the left-hand needle under the horizontal strand of yarn running between the last stitch on the right-hand needle and the first stitch on the left-hand needle.

2 Put the right-hand needle knitwise into the back of the loop formed by the picked-up strand and knit the loop in the same way you would knit a stitch, but through the back loop (see page 139). You have increased by one stitch.

Knit in front and back of next stitch (kfb)
This creates an extra stitch, so it is also sometimes abbreviated as "inc" in a knitting pattern. There will be a visible bar of yarn across the base of the extra stitch.

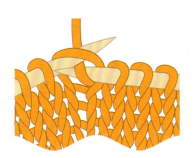 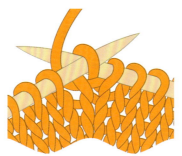 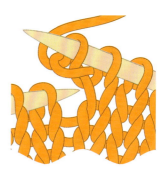

1 Knit the next stitch on the left-hand needle in the usual way, but do not slip the original stitch off the left-hand needle.

2 Move the right-hand needle behind the left-hand needle and put it into the same stitch again, but through the back of the stitch this time. Knit the stitch through the back loop (see page 139).

3 Slip the original stitch off the left-hand needle. You have increased by one stitch.

Decreasing

Slip, slip, knit (ssk)
This method is also quite a common way of creating a slope toward the left. It is abbreviated in patterns as "ssk."

 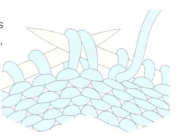

1 Slip the first two stitches knitwise (see opposite) from the left to the right needle, one at a time.

2 Insert the left needle across the front of these two stitches, from left to right as shown, then knit them together.

techniques 137

Knit 2 together (k2tog)

The most straightforward of all the decreases, this simply involves inserting the right needle into two stitches rather than one, from front to back, and knitting as though they were one stitch. The top loop of the resulting stitch leans slightly toward the right, and therefore this technique should be used at the left-hand edge of the shaping, to create a slope inward from left to right. It is abbreviated as "k2tog."

Purl 2 together (p2tog)

You can also purl two stitches together in the same way: insert the right needle into two stitches instead of one, and purl them as if they were one stitch. This stitch also leans toward the right, creating a slope inward from left to right. It is abbreviated as "p2tog."

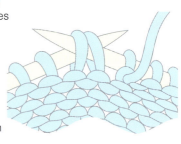

Center double decrease: slip 2 stitches, knit 1 stitch, pass slipped stitches over

Occasionally you may want to work decreases in the center of a piece, in which case you may wish to avoid any directional slant. You can only achieve this when working two decreases at a time.

This method places the center stitch of the three that are worked together on top, and therefore maintains a straight look to the work. It is abbreviated as "sl 2, k1, psso" or "CDD."

1 Work along the row as far as the stitch before the center. Insert the right needle into the next two stitches on the left needle, as if you were about to k2tog. Instead, slip them onto the right needle and do not knit them.

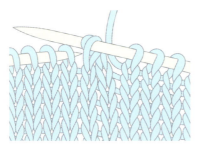

2 Knit the next stitch as normal, then lift the two slipped stitches over the knitted stitch and off the left needle. You should find that the center stitch lies on top of the decreases and has made a straight central column.

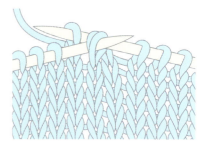

Bind (cast) off

You will need to bind (cast) off the stitches to complete the projects and stop the knitting unraveling.

1 Knit the first two stitches of the next row as usual. Insert the tip of the left needle into the first stitch worked on the right needle, from left to right and at the front of the work. Lift this stitch over the last stitch on the right needle, and drop it off the tip. You will have one stitch remaining on the right needle.

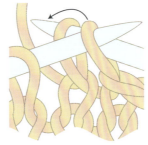

2 Knit one more stitch from the left needle as normal so that you again have two stitches on the right needle, then repeat step 1 again.

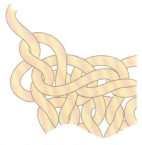

3 Repeat until you have only one stitch left on the right needle and none on the left needle. Pull a long loop of yarn, then remove the right needle, cut the yarn, and thread the end through the loop, tightening it to close.

138 techniques

3-needle bind (cast) off

This is a method of binding (casting) off two edges together, creating a smooth, neat seam. You will need a third needle the same size as the needles the pieces are on.

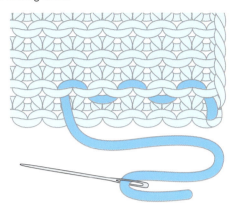

Place both pieces with right sides together, holding both needles together in your left hand with the tips pointing in the same direction. Put the tip of the third needle into the first stitch on each of the other two needles from front to back and knit them as one stitch. Repeat with the second stich on both needles, then use the tip of one of the left-hand needles to lift the first stitch over the second. Repeat until you have one stitch left, then fasten off in the usual way.

Weaving in ends

This technique takes its name from the "weaving" motion worked as you sew the yarn tails in and out of the stitches on the wrong side.

Use a large-eyed knitter's yarn needle (or a tapestry needle), which has a blunt tip to weave the yarn end in and out of a few stitches—the end is shown here in a contrast color for clarity.

Gauge (tension) square

The gauge (tension) is given as the number of stitches and rows needed to produce a 4-in (10-cm) square of knitting.

Using the recommended yarn and needles, cast on 8 stitches more than the gauge instruction asks for. Working in pattern, work 8 rows more than needed. Bind (cast) off loosely. Lay the swatch flat without stretching it. Lay a ruler across the stitches with the 2in (5cm) mark centered on the knitting, then put a pin in the knitting at the 0 and at the 4in (10cm) mark. Count the number of stitches between the pins. Repeat the process across the rows to count the number of rows to 4in (10cm).

If the number of stitches and rows you've counted is the same as the number asked for, you have the correct gauge. If you do not have the same number then you will need to change your gauge by changing the size of your knitting needles. A good rule of thumb is that one difference in needle size will create a difference of one stitch in the gauge. Use larger needles to achieve fewer stitches and smaller ones to achieve more stitches.

If you are knitting in a different yarn to that suggested in the pattern, you may need to knit on thinner or thicker needles than stated on the yarn's ball band to achieve the right gauge.

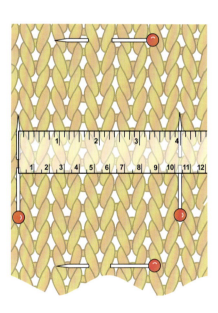

Working through the back loop

You usually knit or purl stitches by putting the right-hand needle into the front of the stitch. However, sometimes a stitch needs to be twisted to create an effect or to work a technique, and to do this you knit or purl into the back of it. This is called working "through the back loop" and is abbreviated to "tbl" in a knitting pattern.

Knitting tbl
Put the right-hand needle into the back of the next stitch on the left-hand needle. Knit the stitch in the usual way, but through the back loop.

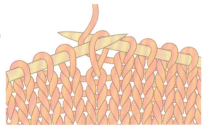

Purling tbl
Put the right-hand needle into the next stitch on the left-hand needle. Purl the stitch in the usual way, but through the back loop.

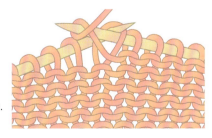

techniques 139

German short rows (slds = slip 1 stitch, make double stitch)

This technique involves turning the knitting before you get to the end of the row, to make a shorter row within the piece. If you do this over and over again, turning at specific points, you can create a variety of effects and shapes.

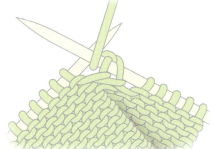

1 When working German Short Rows, work to the turning point, then turn the work so you're ready to work the next row. Slip the first stitch from the left needle to the right needle with the yarn in front. Then pull the working yarn over the right needle to the back of the work (the stitch will now look like a strange double stitch).

2 Move the working yarn into position for the next stitch. In this case, the yarn is brought, between the needles, to the front for purling. Then work as directed in your pattern.

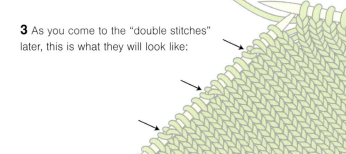

3 As you come to the "double stitches" later, this is what they will look like:

4 When you come to the "double stitches," just knit or purl the strands together as one stitch. Here, the strands are being knitted together.

I-cord

You knit these cords on two double-pointed needles. The number of stitches can vary, depending on how chunky you want the i-cord to be, and a firm tension works best.

1 Cast on as many stitches as needed: here there are four. *Slide the stitches to the right-hand end of the double-pointed needle, with the working yarn on the left of the cast-on row. Pull the yarn tightly across the back of the stitches and knit the first stitch as firmly as you can, then knit the remaining stitches.

2 Repeat from * until the i-cord is the length you need. After the first couple of rows, it will be easy to pull the yarn neatly across the back of the stitches for an invisible join in the cord.

140   techniques

Joining new yarn

You will usually bring in a new ball of yarn or new color (as directed in the pattern or chart) at the beginning of the row/round.

1 Break the old yarn, leaving about a 4–6in (10–15cm) tail. Insert the needle into the next stitch to be knitted, then knit in the new color as usual, leaving a 4–6in (10–15cm) tail.

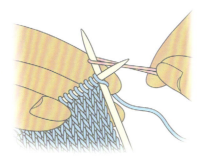

2 The tails can be tied together to hold them in position and to stop the loose stitch from falling off the needle. It's best to knit one or two stitches before tying them in place. Never tie in a double knot, because this will make it difficult to sew in the end later and the knot will eventually work itself out of your work.

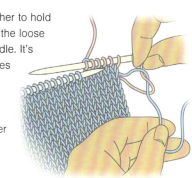

Color knitting using intarsia

Intarsia is a method of color knitting used for motifs rather than for overall patterns. It is used for the chimpanzee (page 46), ring-tailed lemur (page 50), koala (page 65), whale (page 90), toucan (page 116), and owl (page 124). You need a separate ball of yarn for each area of color. It's vital to twist the yarns in the right way to link the areas of color and avoid holes appearing in the knitting, so if this is a new technique for you, practice on a swatch before starting a project.

Vertical color change for intarsia

Don't rush adjusting and linking the yarns on straight vertical color changes as the stitches can become loose.

On a purl row, work to the last stitch in the old color (pink in this example). Bring the new color (gray in this example) from under the old color and purl the next stitch firmly. The same principle applies on a knit row. Work to the last stitch in the old color, then bring the new color under the old color and purl the next stitch firmly.

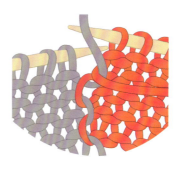

Color change on a slant for intarsia

Where the color change runs in a sloping line, you need to be careful that the yarns are properly linked around one another at the change.

1 On a knit row, work to the last stitch in the old color (gray in this example). Put the left-hand needle knitwise into this stitch, then bring the new color (pink in this example) across under the old color, wrap it around the tip of the right-hand needle, and knit the stitch in the new color.

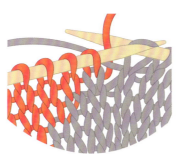

2 On a purl row, work to the last stitch in the new color (pink in this example). Put the left-hand needle purlwise into the next stitch on the left-hand needle, then bring the old color (gray in this example) up under the new color and purl the stitch in the old color.

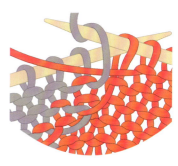

techniques

Color knitting using Fair Isle

Fair Isle involves changing colors to create a design and carrying yarn across the back of the work. This technique is used for the giraffe (page 24). If you haven't tried Fair Isle knitting before, then it's a good idea to try it out on swatches before starting a project, as getting the gauge (tension) of the yarns right with the stranding can take a bit of practice. These instructions are for the simplest method of stranding, where you work holding one yarn at a time. You twist the yarns together before dropping one and changing to the next to avoid creating a hole.

Changing color on a knit row for Fair Isle
It's important to swap the yarns in the right way when changing colors to keep the fabric flat and smooth.

1 Knit the stitches in color A (brown in this example), bringing the yarn across over the strand of color B (lime in this example) to wrap around the needle.

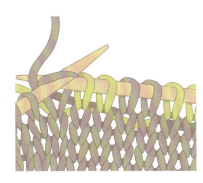

2 At the color change, drop color A and pick up color B, bringing it across under the strand of color A to wrap around the needle. Be careful not to pull it too tight. Knit the stitches in color B. When you change back to color A, bring it across over the strand of color B.

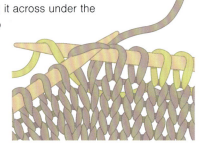

Changing color on a purl row for Fair Isle
You can clearly see how the colors are swapped when working the purl rows.

1 Knit the stitches in color A (brown in this example), bringing the yarn across over the strand of color B (lime in this example) to wrap around the needle.

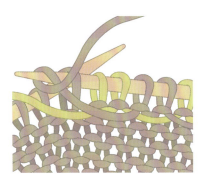

2 At the color change, drop color A and pick up color B, bringing it under the strand of color A to wrap around the needle. Be careful not to pull it too tight. Knit the stitches in color B. When you change back to color A, bring it across over the strand of color B.

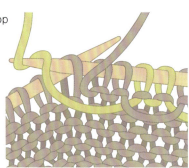

Embroidery

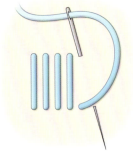

Straight stitch
Bring the needle through to the surface of the fabric and then take it back down to create a small straight stitch.

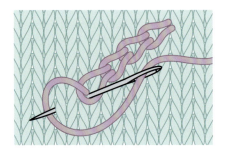

Chain stitch
Bring the needle up through the fabric, then insert it in the same place and bring it up again a bit further along. Loop the end of the yarn around the needle tip before pulling through.

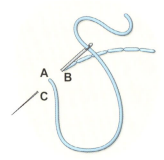

Backstitch
Bring the needle up at A, take it back down one stitch length behind this point at B, and bring it up again at C, one stitch length in front of the point at which it first emerged. Repeat as required.

Adding safety eyes

Note: If you're making a project for a young child, instead of adding safety eyes, embroider the eyes on using a few small straight stitches (see opposite) worked closely together.

Insert each eye from the front of the piece and make sure both eyes are completely level and sitting on the same row before you secure the safety catches at the back. The flat piece of the safety catch is pushed towards the knitted piece from the inside.

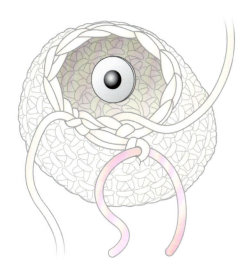

Abbreviations

approx = approximately
CC = contrast color
CDD = center double decrease
cont = continue
dec = decreas(e)ing
DPN = double-pointed needles
beg = begin(ing)
foll = follow(s)ing
inc = increas(e)ing
k = knit
kfb = knit into front and back of stitch
k2tog = knit 2 stitches together
LH = left hand
MC = main color
M1 = make 1 stitch
p = purl
p2tog = purl 2 stitches together

PM = place marker
rem = remaining
rep = repeat
RH = right hand
RM = remove marker
RS = right side
sl = slip
SM = slip marker
ssk = slip, slip, knit
st st = stockinette (stocking) stitch
tbl = through back loop
tog = together
WS = wrong side
wyib = with yarn at the back
wyif = with yarn at the front
yb = yarn back
yf = yarn forward

Special abbreviations

MB (make bobble): Kfb, turn, p2, turn, k2, slip second st from end of needle over first st. (1 st)

T2F (twist 2 front): K second stitch on LH needle, without removing st from needle, k first st on LH needle, slip both sts to RH needle. This will produce a twist to the right.

T2B (twist 2 back): K second st on LH needle through back loop, without removing st from needle, k first st on LH needle, slip both sts to RH needle. This will produce a twist to the left.

Acknowledgments

Thank you to everyone who has helped this book come together.

When I am working on a new project I rely on my children to tell me if it looks "right." Usually, they pick up on something that I wasn't sure about—maybe the position of ears or the shape of the animal needs some work—so thank you to them, especially Lola.

My wonderful friend Lucy has been a great help as always, coming up with ideas and the most amazing facts about some of the animals.

The team at CICO Books have been amazing to work with, unpicking my instructions to form neat and easy-to-read knitting patterns. Thank you to my editor Jenny, and Marie and Marilyn, who bore the brunt of this. Thank you also to the photographer and stylist who have really brought my projects to life.

A note on yarns

The yarns I use are very important to me and often inspire the project. I have used Rico Ricorumi for many of the projects as it comes in a huge range of colors and ⅞oz (25g) balls, the ideal size for these projects.

I have also used Rowan Felted Tweed, mainly because of the texture and tiny flecks of color which really add to the designs.

index

abbreviations 143
axolotl 99–101

backstitch 142
back loop, working through the 139
bat 112–15
bears
  brown bear 44–7
  polar bear 80–3
binding off 138–9
birds
  flamingo 76–9
  owl 124–7
  parrot 128–31
  pelican 120–3
  penguin 84–6
  toucan 116–19
brown bear 44–7

cable method, casting on 133
camel 12–14
casting off 138–9
casting on 133–4
chain stitch (embroidery) 142
chameleon 38–40
chimpanzee 48–51
clown fish 108–9
color knitting
  Fair Isle 142
  Intarsia 141
Continental method
  knit stitch 135
  purl stitch 136
crocodile 87–9

decreasing stitches 137–8

elephant 8–11
embroidery techniques 142
eyes 143

faces 4
Fair Isle knitting 142
flamingo 76–9
frog 96–8

gauge 139
German short rows 140
giraffe 24–7

hippo 93–5

i-cord
  casting on 134
  knitting 140
increasing stiches 137
Intarsia knitting 141

joining new yarn 141

kangaroo 15–19
knit stitch
  Continental method 135
  US/UK method 134
knitting techniques 132–43
koala 67–9

legs 4
lion 30–3

mouths 4

needles, holding 132

octopus 104–5
orang-utan 41–3
owl 124–7

panda 56–9
parrot 128–31
pelican 120–3
penguin 84–6
polar bear 80–3
purl stitch
  Continental method 136
  US/UK method 135

reindeer 70–3
reverse stockinette (stocking) stitch 136
ring-tailed lemur 52–5

safety eyes, adding 143
scarlet king snake 34–5
seahorse 106–7
slipknot, casting on 133
slipping stitches 136
sloth 64–6
starfish 102–3
stockinette (stocking) stitch 136

straight stitch (embroidery) 142
stuffing 4

techniques 132–43
tension 139
tiger 60–3
tortoise 28–9
toucan 116–19

US/UK method
  knit stitch 134
  purl stitch 135

weaving in ends 139
whale 90–2

yarn
  choices for the projects 143
  choosing your own 4
  holding 132
  joining new yarn 141

zebra 20–3

Suppliers

We cannot cover all stockists here, so please explore the knitting stores in your country. If you wish to substitute a different yarn for the one recommended in the pattern, try Yarnsub for suggestions: www.yarnsub.com.

Sue Stratford Knits
Patterns, kits, and yarns
suestratford.co.uk

Rico yarns
rico-design.de

Rowan yarns
www.knitrowan.com

USA
Knitting Fever Inc.
Online sales
www.knittingfever.com

LoveCrafts
Online sales
www.lovecrafts.com

Michaels
Retail stores and online sales
www.michaels.com

WEBS
Online sales
www.yarn.com

UK
Hobbycraft
Retail stores and online sales
www.hobbycraft.co.uk

John Lewis
Retail stores and online sales
www.johnlewis.com

Laughing Hens
Online sales
Tel: +44 (0) 1829 740903
www.laughinghens.com

LoveCrafts
Online sales
www.lovecrafts.com

Wool Warehouse
Online sales
www.woolwarehouse.co.uk

Wool
Yarn, tools
Store in Bath
Tel: +44 (0)1225 469144
www.woolbath.co.uk

Australia
Black Sheep Wool 'n' Wares Retail
Retail store and online sales
www.blacksheepwool.com.au